LOVING JESUS

Loving Jesus

Mother Teresa
edited by
José Luis González-Balado

Servant Publications
Ann Arbor, Michigan

Published by Servant Publications
P.O. Box 8617
Ann Arbor, Michigan 48107

This collection of addresses, comments, interviews, and a
biographical sketch of Agnes Bojaxhiu, known as Mother
Teresa of Calcutta, was edited by José Luis González-
Balado in Spanish and then translated into English by
Susana Labastida.

Cover design by Michael Andaloro
Cover painting by James Adams

    93 94   10 9 8 7 6 5
Printed in the United States of America
ISBN 0-89283-676-8

Contents

Publisher's Preface

THIS BOOK GATHERS TOGETHER recent addresses, speeches, sayings, and comments, of Mother Teresa of Calcutta, the dynamic and unpredictable founder of the Missionaries of Charity. It also includes a biographical sketch of Mother Teresa, pinpointing important dates and developments in her life.

In *Loving Jesus* Mother Teresa eloquently expresses the call to serve the poorest of the poor with the love of Christ. The poor, she says, are those who suffer spiritually or physically in our own families and neighborhoods. Mother Teresa speaks of the lack of love in modern family life, the tragedy of abortion, society's need to care for abandoned and unwanted children, the plight of lepers in Third World countries, and the scourge of AIDS—which she calls "the leprosy of the West."

Loving Jesus also includes an interview with Mother Teresa, probing her reasons for dedicating herself to the poorest of the poor. It provides an informative overview to the woman and her life's work as the founder of the Missionaries of Charity.

The material in *Loving Jesus* has been edited by José Luis González-Balado. Chapter notes are provided at the back of the book, citing the sources for the material included in each chapter. The interview has been included in full in chapter nineteen.

Although many Scripture references have been provided by the editor, the reader should note that Mother Teresa rarely quotes directly from the Bible or cites references when she speaks before an audience. Yet her paraphrases of Scripture and other religious works remain true to the meaning of the original text. Frequently, the paraphrases are taken from popular texts that will be familiar to most readers. The Scripture references are provided for those who wish to reflect on the exact verses in Scripture which Mother Teresa has paraphrased.

Further, the reader should note that Mother Teresa often repeats examples or illustrations in her addresses or interviews. But she always tailors them to suit the topic, the audience, and the occasion—many times rendering an already familiar illustration with fresh insight and meaning.

Finally, the meaning of Mother Teresa's statements should be considered carefully by the reader. The context of her statements is always an unflagging commitment to Christ and his church, along with her special mission to serve the poorest of the poor. Without that understanding, the reader may, at times, misconstrue the meaning of her simple and forthright statements about serving Christ in the poor or some other critical issue, such as care of abandoned and unwanted children.

As you read this book, we hope that the simple yet profound words of Mother Teresa may inspire you to serve those in your midst with the love of Christ.

ONE

God's Love in Action

IT DOES NOT MATTER who we are, it does not matter what our profession is, in other words, what we do. It does not matter what our nationality is, or whether we are rich or poor. Whatever our state in life, above all we are children of God, the work of his hands.

Each one of us will have to face him at the hour of death, and he is going to judge us.

How?

He is going to say, "I was hungry, and you gave me to eat; I was naked, and you clothed me; I was homeless, and you took me in" (Mt 25:35-40).

I may know very little about where you live. I don't know whether you have many people who are hungry for a piece of bread, but I believe yours is a rich country materially, at least as compared to many others in the world.

But if you allow abortion in your country, then you are a very poor country spiritually, so poor that you are afraid of children. You are so afraid of bringing unborn children into the world that you decide they must die.

We live in a world where there is hunger, not only for a piece of bread, but also for love. People feel unwanted, unloved, uncared for. Why? We are too busy. We have no time even to smile at each other.

We have even less time to pray together.

We have even less time to stay together, to satisfy the need we have for each other's company.

DO YOU KNOW THE POOR?

Nakedness is not only the need for a piece of clothing. Nakedness is the need for human dignity which people sometimes lose, which we unjustly take away from the poor. We think they are useless and hopeless. We have so many adjectives for poor people! That is the real nakedness of our world today.

Nakedness is being thrown away by society, unwanted, deserted. That man, that woman, that child—it does not matter who—is unwanted and thrown away.

Some time ago I visited parts of Tokyo, and I found lonely, unwanted people. That is a terrible form of nakedness to me, that is a homelessness of the heart and spirit.

I don't know if you know your own poor.

Maybe there are not the same numbers of poor as in Calcutta or other places in the Third World. But even if there is just one, he or she is my brother, my sister. Why should he or she lie in the gutter?

Why should that one brother be unwanted?

Why is there no hand to lift him up?

Why is there no one to take him in?

He may be a drunkard, but he is my brother, abandoned, unwanted, and uncared for. Maybe—just maybe!—he felt so lonely, so unwanted that he had to take something to drink in order to forget.

That is why I ask you, let us pray that we come to know the poor right in our midst.

The poor may be in our own families. Maybe you have plenty to eat. Maybe you have wonderful things and beautiful houses. But what if your father, your mother, your wife, your husband, or your child feels lonely?

Are you aware of that loneliness?

They may feel unwanted, but you may be so busy you have no time even to smile at your own child, at your husband, or at your wife.

Then there is poverty right in your family!

If you want that to change, you must bring prayer into your family life. You must pray, if you want to be able to love. Whatever way you know how to pray, you must pray.

We all know that there is God who loves us, who has made us. We can turn and ask him, "My Father, help me now. I want to be holy, I want to be good, I want to love."

Holiness is not a luxury for the few; it is not just for some people. It is meant for you and for me, for all of us. It is a simple duty, because if we learn to love, we learn to be holy.

But if we want to be able to love, we must pray! Prayer will give us a clean heart, and a clean heart can see God. If we see God, immediately God's love works in us. And we need to love not with words, but with deeds!

LOVE IN ACTION

I have been told in more than one place, "If you have to give birth to a child, you have to pay so much. And if you have an abortion, you won't have to pay anything."

My sisters and I, we want to save that child. We will help that woman to bring her pregnancy to term and give birth to that child. We will pay whatever it costs. We will make the necessary sacrifices in order to pay.

I have sent word to all the police stations, clinics, and hospitals, "Please don't destroy any child. I will take any child, any time, night or day. Just let me know and I will come for him." Our homes for children are overflowing.

And what a wonderful gift of God is seen when a child is loved and cared for! God's blessing is evident in such beautiful work. It is so beautiful that we have many families that adopt these children we care for. So we are bringing joy into the homes of those who have no children, who cannot have children. We are giving a father's and a mother's love to a child who would have been destroyed.

See the wonderful ways of God! This is really love in action!

TWO

The Family and the Poor

W E READ IN SCRIPTURE that God speaks of his love for us, "I have loved you with an everlasting love" (Jer 31:3).[1]

And he also says, "I have called you by your name. You are mine. The waters will not drown you. Fire will not burn you. I will give up nations for you. You are precious to me. I love you. Even if a mother could forget her child, I will not forget you. I have carved you on the palm of my hand. You are precious to me. I love you" (Is 43:1-4; 49:15-16).

These are the words of God himself for you, for me, for everyone, even for the poorest of the poor. For he has created us for greater things: to love and to be loved. He wants us to love one another as he loves us.

Let us stop for a moment to think about the tenderness of God's love for us. There are thousands of people who would love to have what you have. And yet God has chosen you to be where you are today to share the joy of loving others.

To make this love more real, more loving, more living, he gives himself as the Bread of Life. He gives us his own life. He wants us to love one another, to give ourselves to each other until it hurts. It does not matter how much we give, but how much love we put into our giving.

In the Constitution of the Missionaries of Charity, we have a beautiful part which speaks of the tenderness of Christ, and also of his faithful friendship and love.

To make that love more living, more sure, more tender, Jesus gives us the Eucharist. This is why it is necessary for every Missionary of Charity to feed upon the Eucharist in order to be a true carrier of God's love. She must live on the Eucharist and have her heart and life woven with the Eucharist. No Missionary of Charity can give Jesus if she does not have Jesus in her heart.

GIVING UNTIL IT HURTS

I will tell you a story. One night a man came to our house and told me, "There is a family with eight children. They have not eaten for days." I took some food with me and went.

When I came to that family, I saw the faces of those little children disfigured by hunger. There was no sorrow or sadness in their faces, just the deep pain of hunger.

I gave the rice to the mother. She divided the rice in two, and went out, carrying half the rice. When she came back, I asked her, "Where did you go?" She gave me this simple answer, "To my neighbors—they are hungry also!"

Her neighbors were Muslims. I was not surprised that she gave, because poor people are really very generous. But I was surprised that she knew they were hungry. As a rule, when we are suffering, we are so focused on ourselves we have no time for others. This woman showed something of the truly generous love of Christ.

The greatness of the poor is something beautiful. Months ago in New York, one of our AIDS patients called me and said, "I want to tell you something very private, because you are my friend. When my headache becomes unbearable—this disease gives terrible headaches—I compare it with the pain Jesus must have had with the crown of the thorns. When the pain moves to my back, I compare it with the pain Jesus had to bear when they whipped him. When my hands ache, I compare it with the pain Jesus felt when they crucified him.''

There you have an example of the greatness of love in the love of this young man, the victim of such a terrible disease. He had no hope of surviving. And yet see how he loved! He found the courage and strength to pray to Jesus and share his suffering with Christ himself.

There was no sign of sadness or distress on his face. He was radiating peace and joy. He only asked me, ''Please take me home!'' (They call our house ''home.'') I brought him to our home and took him to Jesus in the chapel.

I had never had the chance of seeing anybody speak to Jesus on the cross as I saw that sick young man speak to Christ. I believe there was a tender conversation between Jesus and him.

After three days, that young man died. He had been in jail for terrible crimes, yet he died with a purified heart.

See the tenderness of God, taking him out of

there and giving that young man the joy of belonging only to him. See also the greatness of the poor!

TO CONSOLE JESUS

It is good for us to focus on our Lord and ask ourselves, "Do I really love Jesus like that? Do I really accept the joy[2] of loving by sharing in his passion?" Because even today Jesus is looking for somebody to console and comfort him.

You remember what happened in Gethsemane: Jesus was longing for somebody to share in his agony. The same thing happens in our lives. Can he share his sorrow with us?

Are you there to comfort him?
He comes to you in the hungry.
He comes to you in the naked.
He comes to you in the lonely.
He comes to you in the drunkard.
He comes to you in the prostitute.
He comes to you in the street person.
He may come to you in the lonely father, or mother, or sister, or brother in your own family.
Are you willing to share the joy of his love with them?

That is why we need the Eucharist, to share the joy of loving Jesus. That is why we need a deep life of prayer. So let us ask Our Lady to teach us how to pray.

You are called to pray, to be alone with Jesus. I haven't the slightest doubt that if your hearts are clean, you will surely hear the voice of God in your heart.

He is asking for something. "I looked for one to comfort me, and I found no one" (Ps 69:21). Let's allow Jesus to find us!

Nothing and no one will ever separate you from the love of Christ. Let's go home with a firm decision: "I will love Jesus with an undivided love!"

Who will help you to do that? Our Lady! Remember the story of Jesus, his disciples, and his mother at the marriage feast at Cana when the wine ran out (Jn 2:1-11)? Our Lady told the servants, "Do whatever he [Jesus] tells you!" Today, in this gathering, again Our Lady is saying to us, "Do whatever Jesus tells you!"

Take love, peace, and joy into the heart of your family! Love begins at home. And when you share that love, it will bring peace into your midst as well.

Suffering will never be completely absent from our lives. Through it, we are given the chance to share the joy of loving Jesus in his passion—it is beautiful to think of that!

So don't be afraid of suffering. Your suffering, too, is a great means of love, if you make use of it, especially if you offer it for peace in the world.

The Holy Father, who understands suffering, came to India. He wanted to come to Calcutta to see our home for the dying. When he arrived, he made the rounds and blessed every patient. (All our patients are from the street.) Many were dying and sick and in great pain.

The Holy Father also wanted to see our mortuary. He went inside, and touched every dead body as a sign of blessing and reverence for the dead.

The place where we have our home is a completely Hindu area. We are the only Catholics there. Yet when the people saw the Holy Father, they said, "A man of God came among us!"

His presence had brought so much peace and joy and love to our people. This is the greatness of God's love when it shines in a person.

LOVE BEGINS BY PRAYING TOGETHER

Where does that love begin?
In our families.
And how does it begin?

By praying together.
The family that prays together, stays together.
And if you stay together, you will love one another as Jesus loves each person in your family.

Make sure that in the beautiful place where you live no child, no man, no woman feels unwanted or unloved. If you find somebody who feels that way, open your doors, open your hearts to them.

Resist the great destroyer of peace. Abortion has become the greatest destroyer of peace. It destroys love. It destroys the image of God. It destroys the presence of God. It destroys the conscience of the mother.

Let us pray that God will save all the beautiful countries of the world through his love. In every country, you will find great people among the poor. Love them. Pray for them.

I will pray for you and your children. I will pray for you to grow in holiness. Jesus has said very clearly, "Be holy as the Father in Heaven is holy!"

Be only for Jesus through the intercession and help of Mary. Be in your family one heart full of love in the heart of Jesus through Mary who is your spiritual mother.

THE TROUBLE WITH THE MODERN FAMILY

I think the world today is upside-down. It is suffering so much because there is so little love in the home and in family life.

We have no time for our children.

We have no time for each other.

There is no time to enjoy each other.

Love lives in homes, and the lack of love causes so much suffering and unhappiness in the world today.

Everybody today seems to be in such a terrible rush, anxious for greater development and greater riches, so that children have very little time for their parents. And parents have very little time for their children and for each other.

So the breakdown of peace in the world begins at home.

People who really and truly love each other are the happiest people in the world. We see that with our very poor people. They love their children and they love their families. They may have very little, in fact, they may not have anything, but they are happy people.

Jesus did not say, "Love the whole world."

He said, "Love one another."

You can only love one person at a time. If you

look at the numbers, you get lost. While you are talking about hunger, somebody is dying next to you.

If you want to do something beautiful for God, look at your own family and at the poor around you.

It is a gift from God for you to be able to serve him in your families and in his poor. Even if it is one person only, that one is still your brother or your sister.

Nationality doesn't matter.

Color doesn't matter.

Being rich or poor doesn't matter.

That person is your brother or your sister.

And how do we know this? Because Jesus said, "Whatever you do for the least of my brethren, you do to me" (Mt 25:40).

THREE

Our Life with Christ

JESUS, BEING RICH, became poor for you and for me. I don't think we could have ever loved God if Jesus never became one of us. So that we might be able to love God, he himself became one of us in all things, except sin.

It was not enough for him to become poor like us. He made himself the Bread of Life. And he said, "Unless you eat my flesh and drink my blood, you cannot live, you cannot have eternal life" (Jn 6:52, 54).

Think of it! Bread—even a little child can eat it.

This is the humility of God, the poverty he chose by becoming one of us. He made himself the Bread of Life to satisfy our hunger for love. If we have been created in the image of God, then we have been created to love, because God is love. We have been created for great things.

THE DISTRESSING DISGUISE
OF JESUS IN THE POOR

This is why the crippled and blind, the lepers, the unwanted and the unloved are our brothers and sisters.[1]

See the goodness of God! It was not enough for him to feed us, to make himself one of us. He had to satisfy his own hunger for us:

So he makes himself the hungry one.
He makes himself the naked one.
He makes himself the homeless one.

And he said, "Whatever you did for the least of these my brethren, you did it to me. For I was hungry and you gave me to eat" (Mt 25:40).

Jesus, in the least of his brethren, is not only hungry for a piece of bread, but hungry for love, to be known, to be taken into account.

He is not only lacking a piece of clothing, he is stripped of human dignity. Very often, through injustice, we take human dignity away from the poor! Or the poor may have been robbed of chastity, purity of soul and body.

Jesus is the homeless one. He is not only lacking a house made of bricks or wood. He is suffering the terrible loneliness of being homeless, a more terrifying disease than leprosy, tuberculosis, AIDS, or any other disease a human body can bear. The disease of being unloved and unwanted, of having no one to call your own, is a very great poverty and a very harmful disease in our days.

To make sure that we understand what he says, Jesus is going to judge us on love. He is going to judge us on our response to this very beautiful call, "I was hungry and you gave me to eat. Come, the blessed of my Father!" Or, "I was hungry, and you did not give me to eat. Go, I do not know you!"

You and I will have to face that one day. But it is not necessary for us to be afraid of Jesus. Let this be our response today:

If we really understand the Eucharist,
if we really center our lives on Jesus' body and blood,
if we nourish our lives with the bread of the Eucharist,
it will be easy for us to see Christ in that hungry one next door,
the one lying in the gutter,
that alcoholic man we shun,
our husband or our wife, or our restless child.
For in them, we will recognize the distressing disguises of the poor: Jesus in our midst.

Do I recognize Christ in a distressing disguise?

Right in my own home!
In the very heart of my family!
There is no need for me even to leave the house.
What about the elderly—my own father, my own mother?
Do I recognize Jesus in them?
Do they seem like a burden as they grow older?
Am I capable of bearing their pain?
Am I capable of smiling at them?
Are they special to me?

I remember one of our Sisters, who had just graduated from the university. She came from a well-to-do family that lived outside of India.

According to our rule, the very next day after joining our society, the postulants must go to the Home for Dying Destitutes in Calcutta. Before this Sister went, I told her, "You saw the priest during the Mass, with what love, with what delicate care he touched the body of Christ. Make sure you do the same thing when you get to the home, because Jesus is there in a distressing disguise."

So she went, and after three hours, she came back. That girl from the university, who had seen and understood so many things, came to my room with such a beautiful smile on her face. She said, "For three hours I've been touching the body of Christ!"

And I said, "What did you do? What happened?"

She said, "They brought a man from the street who had fallen into a drain and had been there for some time. He was covered with maggots and dirt and wounds. And though I found it very difficult, I cleaned him, and I knew I was touching the body of Christ!"

She knew!

Do we know?

Do we recognize Jesus under the appearance of bread?

If we recognize him under the appearance of bread, we will have no difficulty recognizing him in the disguise of the suffering poor, and the suffering in our family, in our own community.

It is always so much easier for us to be very kind to the people outside our own circle than to be full of smiles and full of love to those in our own homes. For me that means being kind to my own Sisters.

Yesterday is gone.

Tomorrow is yet to come.

We have only today.

If we help our children to be what they should be today, then, when tomorrow becomes today, they will have the necessary courage to face it with greater love.

Right from the very beginning, since love begins at home, I think we should teach our children to love one another at home. They can learn this only from their father and mother, when they see the parents' love for each other.

I think this will strengthen our children, so that they can give that love to others in the future.

THE VALUE OF NATURAL FAMILY PLANNING

It is true, people are very anxious about the future and about over-population. But there is natural family planning. That method can help couples plan their family without destroying God's gift of life.

I think we should train our children for the future by teaching them to respect the dignity of life, by teaching them that life is a gift from

God, something created by him, something to be lived for him. By the purity and sanctity of their lives, they will then be able to face the future using simple, natural means that God has created.

We are, on our part, teaching our poor people natural family planning. We are teaching the young people so that in the future they will know what to do and will protect life.

The poor have told me, "From the time we have been practicing this way of life, our family has remained united, our family is healthy, and we can have a baby whenever we like." All this has brought so much peace and unity into the lives of our poor people.

It is something so wonderful to see: peace in the family, because they are not destroying anything, not killing anything.

By properly using the natural family planning method, couples are using their bodies to glorify God in the sanctity of family life. I think that if we could bring this method to every country, if our poor people would learn it, there would be more peace, more love in the family between parents and children.

People are afraid of having children.

Children have lost their place in the family.

Children are very lonely, very lonely!

When children come home from school, there is no one to greet them. Then they go back to the streets.

We must find our children again and bring them back home.

Mothers are at the heart of the family. Children need their mothers. If the mother is there, the children will be there too. For the family to be whole, the children and the mother also need the father to be present in the home.

I think if we can help to bring them all back together, we will do a beautiful thing for God.

FOUR

We Are the Children of God

L ET US ASK OUR LADY to keep us company, to stay with us.[1] Let us ask Mary, who besides being the Mother of Jesus, is so beautiful, so pure, so immaculate, and full of grace! If Mary stays with us, we can keep Jesus in our hearts, so that we can love and serve him through ministry to the poorest of the poor.

Let us stop for a moment to pray for our parents, for having loved and wanted us, for having given us life.

In the Gospels we read that God so loved the world that he gave us Jesus through the most pure Virgin. As soon as she received the announcement from the angel, Mary went in haste to her cousin Elizabeth, who was with child. And the unborn child John the Baptist rejoiced in Elizabeth's womb. How wonderful it was—Almighty God chose an unborn child to announce the coming of his Son![2]

Yet today, unborn children are targeted for death, persons to be discarded and destroyed. Abortion destroys the image of God. It is the most terrible plague in our society, the greatest killer of love and peace. Those little children still unborn have been created for bigger things: to love and to be loved.

GOD'S GENTLE LOVE FOR US

In the holy Scripture God says to us, "Can a mother forget her child at the breast, or fail to cherish the son of her womb? Yet even if these forget, I will never forget you. See, I have carved you on the palms of my hands, your ramparts are always under my eye (Is 49:16). You are all precious to me. I love you. I have called you by name: you are mine (Is 43:1). The water will not drown you, the fire will not burn you." This delicate love of God is for us all.

I will never forget a man who came to see me a few weeks ago. He said to me, "My only son is dying. The doctor has prescribed a medicine which can only be found in England."

While he was still speaking, another man

came in with a small basket full of medicines. On top of them all was precisely the one that the doctor had prescribed. God in his love provided for that child.

When we look at the Blessed Sacrament, we realize how much Jesus has loved each one of us. We know he made himself the Bread of Life so that we could love each other.

Christ made himself the living bread to show us this love, and to give us a chance to show that same love by loving each other. He says to us, "Love each other as I loved you. As my Father loves me, so I have loved you. Love each other" (Jn 13:34; 15:9).

Where does this love begin? In our homes, when we pray together as families. A family that prays together, stays together. And, if you stay together in Christ, then you will love each other as God desires.

To make it easier for us to love each other, Jesus has told us, "Whatever you do for the least of my brethren, you do it to me. When you receive a child in my name, you are receiving me" (Lk 9:48). "When you give a glass of water to somebody in my name, you give it to me" (Mk 9:41).

This is the love Jesus has brought to earth.

This is the love we must show to each other.

Why? Because he loved us first.

"Precisely because of the love that you will have for each other, they will recognize that you are my disciples, that you are Christians" (Jn 13:35).

The other day, two friends of mine came to see me. They brought me a large amount of money to use for feeding the poor. (You must know that just in Calcutta we feed around nine thousand people daily.)[3] I asked them, "Where did you get all that money?"

They answered, "We were married two days ago, but before that we had decided not to have a large wedding banquet. As a witness of our love for each other, we wanted to bring this money to Mother Teresa."

This is the greatness of young people! They are so generous! I asked them further, "Why did you do this?"

They answered, "We love each other so very much, that we wanted to share our love with other people, especially with those you are serving."

We should ask ourselves, "Have I really experienced the joy of loving?"

True love is love that causes us pain, that hurts, and yet brings joy. That is why we must pray to God and ask him to give us the courage to love.

He who has a pure heart shows God to us and helps us to discover God in our neighbors. And then it does not matter to which political party one belongs, the color of one's skin, the language one speaks; we are all brothers and sisters.

In 1985, the government of Communist China invited me to visit that country. A Communist leader asked me, "What is a Communist for you?"

I answered him, "Someone called to be a child of God, my brother, my sister."

We are here to be witnesses of love and to celebrate life, because life has been created in the image of God. Life is to love and to be loved.

That is why we all have to take a strong stand so that no child—boy or girl—will be rejected or unloved. Every child is a sign of God's love, that has to be extended over all the earth.

If you hear of someone who does not want to have her child, who wants to have an abortion, try to convince her to bring the child to me. I will love that child, who is a sign of God's love.

OUR BROTHERS AND SISTERS IN THE MISSIONARIES OF CHARITY

I also wish to thank those parents who have given their sons and daughters to serve our

Lord. That child was the greatest gift God had given to them, and God has generously compensated them with a vocation for his service. Yes, I want to say thanks to these parents.

Our Brothers and Sisters—the Missionaries of Charity—devote themselves in a special way to loving and serving the poorest of the poor. To do this, we take first of all the three vows of chastity (to love the Lord fully, with undivided love), of poverty (to live as the poorest of the poor), and of obedience (to totally surrender ourselves to God).[4] To these, we add a fourth vow which is to give wholehearted, free service to the poorest of the poor.[5]

Pray for us, that we do not spoil the work of God, that this may always be the work of God. Pray for our poor, the old, the unwanted children, the sick, the lepers, for those who suffer from AIDS, for all those we can serve as a gift from God. Let us ask our Lord to grant us the grace to serve our brothers and sisters throughout the world who live and die in poverty and misery.

Lord, give them, today, through our hands, their daily bread! Grant that, through our understanding love, we may bring them peace and joy. Let us never forget that what we do with love always brings peace.

FIVE

In the Very Heart of the World

We, the missionaries of charity, have homes for the sick and dying in many places. We also have children's homes for the unwanted, the unloved, the sick, and the retarded.

God has been just wonderful to us by giving us more parents, especially in India, who want to adopt our children. We have many children ready to be adopted.

People very often make jokes with me (or about me, rather), because we are also teaching natural family planning. They say, "Mother Teresa is doing plenty of talking about family planning, but she herself does not practice it. She is having more and more children every day."

Indeed, that is the way it is. Our homes are always full of children. And as they come, God has been tremendously wonderful to us. We always get plenty of parents who are hungry to give their love and their home to a child. You would be surprised how much love is showered on those unwanted little children, who otherwise would have been destined to live in the gutter.

Lately, I have experienced what a child meant for the family that adopted him. I had given the child to a high-class family. After some time, I heard that the child was sick and completely crippled.

So I sent to the family and said, "Give the child back to me and I will give you a healthy one!"

The father said to me, "Take my life first, before you take this child!"

That shows you what the child meant to that family and how beautifully that little one, in spite of all his suffering, had fit into the lives of those people. These are some of the great things that God is doing with us and through us, with your help.

OUR REHABILITATION CENTERS FOR LEPERS

The Missionaries of Charity take care of many leprosy patients. In order to offer them a new life, with the help of the Indian government we are trying to build rehabilitation centers all over India. Our goal is for the lepers to live a normal life like you and me, where they can feel that they are somebody, that they are our brothers and sisters, human beings created by the same loving hand of God.

The Sisters and the Brothers, to be able to do this work, take a vow of chastity (to love Christ with an undivided love) through the freedom of poverty (you must be free to love Christ), and in total surrender to obedience (because, if we belong to Christ, he must be able to use us).

Our vocation is nothing else but to belong to Christ. The work that we do is only a means to put our love for Christ into living action.

He put his love for us into action by dying on the cross, by making himself the Bread of Life. And so we, too, want to love him by serving, loving, and taking care of the poorest of the poor.

God has blessed our work with many wonderful vocations. We have many young girls who have dedicated their lives to be pure, to serve, to touch Christ in the distressing disguise of the poor.[1]

You will be very surprised to know what these young girls—your own children—write: "I want a life of poverty, prayer, and sacrifice that will lead me to serve the poor." It is beautiful to see how these young people give without counting the cost.

OUR DAILY SCHEDULE

To be able to give life like that, our lives are centered on the Eucharist and prayer. We begin our day with Mass, Holy Communion, and meditation.

Our community life is very closely woven together.[2] We do everything together: we pray together, we eat together, we work together.

Since we have only two saris, we wash one every day.

After Mass and breakfast, some Sisters go to the Home for Dying Destitutes, some to the leper colonies, some to the little schools we have in the slums, some take care of the preparation and distribution of food, some go visit needy families, some go teach catechism, and so on.

They go all over the city (in Calcutta alone, we have fifty-nine centers, the Home for Dying Destitutes is only one center). The Sisters travel everywhere with a rosary in hand. That is the way we pray in the streets. We do not go to the people without praying. The rosary has been our strength and our protection.

We always go in twos, and we come back around 12:30 P.M. At that time we have our lunch. After lunch, very often we have to do housework.

Then, for half an hour, every Sister has to rest, because all the time they are on their feet. After that, we have an examination of conscience, pray the Liturgy of the Hours, and the *Via Crucis*, "Way of the Cross."

At 2 P.M., we have spiritual reading for half an hour, and then a cup of tea.

At 3 P.M., the professed Sisters again go out. (Novices and postulants remain in the house. They have classes in theology and Scripture and other subjects, such as the rules of monastic orders.)

Between 6:15-6:30 P.M., everybody comes back home.

From 6:30 to 7:30 P.M., we have adoration of the Blessed Sacrament. To be able to have this hour of adoration, we have not had to cut back on our work. We can work as many as ten or even twelve hours a day in service to the poor, following this schedule.

At 7:30 P.M., we have dinner.

After dinner, for about twenty minutes, we

have to prepare the work for next morning.

From 8:30 until 9 P.M., we have recreation. Everybody talks at the top of her lungs, after having worked all day long.

At 9 P.M., we go to the chapel for night prayers and to prepare the meditations for the next morning.

Once a week, every week, we have a day of recollection. That day, the first-year novices go out, because they are the ones who don't go out every day. Then all the professed Sisters stay in for the day of recollection. That day we also go to confession and spend more time in adoration of the Blessed Sacrament.

This is time when we can regain our strength and fill up our emptiness again with Jesus. That's why it is a very beautiful day.

The Need for
Holy Priests

S EVERAL YEARS AGO, the president of Yemen
asked me to allow some Sisters to go to that
country. He wanted a home of the Missionaries
of Charity to be established in Yemen.

That country had been deprived of Catholic
priests and nuns for six hundred years. There
were no tabernacles there, no churches, no
parishes! It was a completely Muslim country.

I told the president, "I am willing to allow the
Sisters to go if you give permission for a priest
to go with us. Because without Jesus, we will
not go." And then the president gave us
permission.

I had never before realized the greatness of
the priesthood[1] until I saw it in Yemen. When
the priest came, the altar, the tabernacle, and
Jesus came with him. All those years there had

not been an altar, a tabernacle, or Jesus.

Now we have three houses there,[2] with three tabernacles in them. The people that come to work there use our homes as centers of prayer.

This is the greatness of the priesthood!

WE NEED HOLY PRIESTS

During the 1982 Synod, I asked the Holy Father, "Give us holy priests, and we Sisters and our families will be holy!"

Without priests, we have no Jesus.
Without priests, we have no absolution.
Without priests, we cannot receive Holy Communion.

And so the greatness of the priest becomes apparent.

I had the same experience in Ethiopia. In some places, the missionaries had been expelled and the churches had been closed. I asked the government, "What about the poor people? I am ready to allow the Sisters to come."[3]

They said, "Yes. Let them come."

Then I said, "But we cannot come without priests."

And so a priest came along and again a church was opened.

See the greatness of the priesthood! See how the priest needs to be holy, to be present to give Jesus to our people.

In our congregation now we have Sisters, Brothers, and priests.

In New York we have a home for homeless people, and two hundred people from the streets come every day to eat. We have a chapel with a tabernacle for them. A priest comes in and talks to them a little. Many of these street people have approached the priest and confessed their sins after twenty, thirty, or forty years.

And the same happens at our home for AIDS patients. There is a priest who visits them. Some of these people have been in jail. Many of them are so bitter, so hurt! But some of them have died a beautiful death.

Who taught them to die so peacefully?

The priest!

One day, our Sisters found a man completely alone in a closed-up room.

They went in, they washed his clothes, they cleaned his room, they gave him a bath. He never spoke a word.

After two days, he told the Sisters, "You have

brought God in my life, now bring me a priest also.''

The Sisters brought the priest, and the man made his confession after sixty years. Next morning, he died.

See the greatness of the priestly vocation!

God had come into the life of that old man, but he needed that connection, that priestly hand to wash away his sins with the precious blood of Christ.

How pure the hearts of priests must be to be able to say, ''This is my body.''

How pure their hands must be to grant absolution at any time!

When we go to confession we go as sinners full of sin. And when we come back from confession, we come back as sinners without sin.

How great for priests to have been chosen by Christ to guide our people!

I AM VERY GRATEFUL TO PRIESTS

I pray very often for priests, because we are in seventy-five countries and I see the hunger of the people for God. In many of these countries there are no priests. So we pray a lot for priests to be holy, because people are hungry for God.

I am very grateful to priests because they have done much for our congregation by helping our Sisters live true religious lives. We specially prepare the Thursday evenings before every First Friday, and especially we pray for priests. We have adoration each night and we offer it especially for priests.

The heart of Jesus is in the priest. In choosing a man to be a priest, Jesus has given himself totally to that man. It is only the priest who can give the real living Jesus to us—in the Blessed Sacrament.

It is very important that priests help the people to come close to Jesus. They need to help the people to have clean hearts, because a clean heart is able to see Christ.

I remember when Archbishop Fulton J. Sheen told me that from the day he had been ordained a priest, he had never missed an hour of daily adoration of the Blessed Sacrament.

Up to 1973 we used to have adoration only once a week. In 1973, during the General Chapter of our congregation, there was a unanimous cry, "We want daily adoration of the Blessed Sacrament!"

We have much work to do for the poor. Still we have not had to cut back on our work in order to have that hour of adoration. (Often that is the excuse some people give for not having adoration every day.)

I can tell you I have seen a great change in our congregation from the day we started having adoration every day. Our love for Jesus is more intimate. Our love for each other is more understanding. Our love for the poor is more compassionate. And we have twice as many vocations.

Adoration of the Blessed Sacrament and devotion to the Sacred Heart of Jesus go together. We try to have our lives woven with the Eucharist so that we are more united to the Sacred Heart of Jesus.

More and more young people are coming to our houses for adoration, even in Communist countries where our Sisters are working. Especially in Poland, Yugoslavia, and East Germany, many young people come for adoration. This has changed many, many lives.

In our homes for the dying, we have the Blessed Sacrament. And there is always somebody praying.

The Sacred Heart of Jesus is the focus of our love. The Eucharist is our strength, our joy, our love, and our peace, enabling us to receive Jesus and then share him with others. And the priest is our guide, for the heart of Jesus is in him.

SEVEN

To Be Jesus

HOLY MARY, Mother of Jesus and mother of men and women, give us your immaculate heart, your loving heart so full of humility, and we will receive Jesus, the Bread of Life. We will love him as you loved him.

Through the poor and the social outcasts that he will entrust to us, we will serve Jesus, remembering the following prayer by Cardinal Newman:

Dear Lord, help me to spread your fragrance wherever I go. Flood my soul with your spirit and life. Penetrate and possess my whole being so utterly that all my life may only be a radiance of yours.

Shine through me, and be so in me that every soul I come in contact with may feel your presence in my soul. Let them look up and see no longer me, but only you, oh Lord! Stay

with me, then I shall begin to shine as you do;
so to shine as to be a light to others. The light,
oh Lord, will be all from you; none of it will be
mine; it will be you shining on others
through me. Let me thus praise you in the
way you love best, by shining on those
around me.

Let me preach you without preaching, not
by words but by my example, by the catch-
ing force, the sympathetic influence of what I
do, the evident fullness of the love my heart
bears to you. Amen.[1]

GIVE CHRIST TO THE WORLD

The whole world is hungry for God.

Priests[2] can satisfy that hunger with the
tenderness and love of Christ. They give the
world this Jesus who is inflaming our hearts.

I remember a man who came to us one day.
He went straight to the women's area without
saying a word to me. He stopped next to a Sister
who was caring for a sick woman covered with
maggots and filth. He looked at the hands, face,
and eyes of the Sister, and he suddenly understood that it was the love of God that gave the

Sister strength to do her work.

He then came to me and said, "I had come here full of hate, but now I am leaving with the presence of God in my heart. I have seen God's love in the face of that Sister, caring for the sick woman as if she were caring for Christ himself."

That is the task of a priest: to treat each human being like Jesus and to be his presence in the world.

I say to all priests: Be holy and teach us to become holy also. Teach us prayers that will purify our hearts and help us grow in our faith. Remind us of the importance of meditation on Jesus, our source of love and service.

You, who have consecrated your lives and your hearts, must be poor, chaste, and holy, to be able to say, "This is my body" at the consecration, and to give us this Bread of Life by which we live.

I ask you, I beg you to give all your time to others and fully live your priesthood. Wherever obedience may send you, you must become a living presence of Christ.

We all have been called by God. "I have called you by your name," Jesus said. "You are mine. No harm will come to you. You are precious in my sight. I love you."

God sends you to be his tenderness and love

to his people. If you love Christ, it will be easy for you to fully belong to Jesus and to give Jesus to everyone you find.

I say to all priests: You have not become priests to be social workers.

You must have a life of holiness, and consecrated obedience and poverty. Everything you do must spring from your consecrated life.

Christ offers you his faithfulness and his personal friendship. To make this living unity more beautiful, he gives you the Eucharist to share with others.

The church and the world have never experienced a greater need for holy priests than today. The whole world is watching you. You must bring Jesus to all the divided families, to all the broken homes. You have to teach them all how to adore the Eucharistic Christ and how to pray the rosary. We must again consecrate our families to the Sacred Heart of Jesus, as priests used to do.

Several years ago, with the permission of the Holy See, we started the *Corpus Christi Fraternity for Priests,* with these vows: serious commitment to become holy, to bring Jesus to others, and to take his tenderness and love to each soul one meets.

LET JESUS USE YOU

I say to all priests: Sometimes it may become a burden to hear confessions for long hours, but Jesus did it during his agony on the cross and you must be like Christ. You must allow Jesus to use you without consulting you first. You belong to him, you are his and only his.

The world is not only hungry for bread but for love. You may not see in your country the sick eaten away by worms, but there are other kinds of worms that gnaw at hearts.

One day, I picked up from the rubbish a woman older than I. She kept on repeating that her son had thrown her out of his home. She was suffering much more from her son's lack of love than from the fever which ravished her.

It took me a long time to convince her to say simply before she died, "I forgive my son."

We all want to love God. But how? Jesus made himself the Bread of Life to satisfy our hunger. Then he made himself naked, homeless, destitute, the leper, the AIDS patient, the drug-addict, the prostitute, so that all of us could satisfy his hunger for our love.

Let us pray for all our fellow countrymen and women, and treat them as the beloved children of God. Then God will be with us.

Let us bring Our Lady into our lives by being faithful to the rosary, and we will bring joy, peace, and happiness.

And now, let us ask Our Lady in prayer for our priests:

Mary, Mother of Jesus and mother of all those who share in his priestly ministry, we come to you as children come to their mother.

We ask you to intercede for those called to the priesthood that they may become true men of God. Our human condition is weak, so we come to you for your motherly help, that they may be able to master their weaknesses and become men of strength for your Son.

Pray for them so that they may become men of prayer.

We ask for the love of your Son, so that love may reign and they may become men of mercy and forgiveness. We ask your maternal blessing so that they may be the likeness of your beloved Son, our Lord and Savior Jesus Christ.

As our mother, we place all our trust and our lives in your hands, and beseech you on behalf of our priests. Amen.

As our mother, we place all our trust and our lives in your hands, and beseech you on behalf of our priests. Amen.

EIGHT

The Poor Can Teach Us

OUR RELIGIOUS SISTERS, our religious Brothers, and our lay Missionaries of Charity,[1] but especially our religious Sisters and Brothers, take a vow to give wholehearted, free service to the poorest of the poor as an expression of their love for Christ.

That's why we have homes for the sick and dying, most of whom we pick up off the streets. We have these homes all over the world: in Australia, England, Africa, the Middle East, India, Latin America, Europe, and the United States.

In some places, we don't have a home for dying destitutes, but we have numerous shut-ins whose homes are really homes for the dying—where people die as a number, not as human beings with dignity. When they die, sometimes nobody even knows their names.

THE POOR DON'T NEED OUR SYMPATHY

What great poverty!
Are we aware of that?
Do we know what fear is?
Do we know the lonely?
Do we know the unwanted and the unloved?
Do we know the hungry?
Do we really know what hunger is?

I'll give you an example of what hunger is. A child got a piece of bread from a Sister. (He had not eaten for some time.) I saw that child eating the bread slowly, crumb by crumb. I said to him, "I know you are hungry. Why don't you eat the bread up?"

The little one answered, "I want it to last longer!"

He was afraid that when he finished the bread, his hunger would come back again. And so he ate it crumb by crumb!

The other child next to him, was not even eating. I thought that he had finished his bread. But the little one said, "My father is sick. I'm very hungry, but my father is sick, and I think he would love to have this piece of bread."

That good little child was willing to go without food to be able to give his father the joy of having a little piece of bread.

The poor are great people!

They don't need our sympathy.

They aren't asking us to feel sorry for them.

They are great people!

They deserve our love!

Not long ago, some Sisters and I went out and picked up four or five people off the streets. One of them was in terrible condition, so I told the Sisters, "I'll take care of her." And I tried to do all that I could for her, all that my love of Jesus could do.

When I put her in bed, she took hold of my hand. There was a beautiful smile on her face. She said only, "Thank you!" And then she died.

She gave me much more than I had given her. She gave me her grateful love.

I couldn't help but examine myself. I said, "If I were she, what would I have done?" And my answer was very sincere, "I would have tried to draw some attention to myself by saying, 'I'm hungry, I'm cold, I'm dying!'"

But she had courage, and she had love to give to me, instead of keeping it for herself, instead of being focused on herself. These are very admirable things!

REASON TO BE HAPPY

Why are the Sisters always smiling?

Because we are not social workers.

We are trying to be contemplatives in the heart of the world. We have chosen to be Missionaries of Charity, to be carriers of God's love.

We have no reason to be unhappy.

How can that be?

If the words of Jesus are true, "I was hungry, I was sick, I was naked, I was homeless, and you did it to me," (Mt 25:40) then we are touching him twenty-four hours a day.

So you, in your lives, in your own homes, can be in his presence twenty-four hours a day, if your lives are woven with prayer and sacrifice.

LET US SEEK OUT THE POOR

The call is basically the same for you too, you who have chosen to be Christians. With Jesus and for Jesus, you will be able to live happily.

What we are doing, you cannot do.

And what you are doing, we cannot do.

But together, we are doing something beautiful for God.

If we want to be holy, let us find the poor, first in our own homes and then right next door. May our service to the poor further the salvation of all mankind, of you and me, for we are touching Jesus.

NINE

Sharing
the Good News

WE READ IN THE SCRIPTURES that God so loved the world that he gave his Son Jesus. God gave Jesus to the Virgin Mary, his immaculate mother. When Jesus came into her life, she went with haste to give the joy of Christ's presence to her cousin Elizabeth.

And there, the most wonderful story of an unborn child begins.

It was an unborn child, in Elizabeth's womb, who recognized the presence of Christ in the world. We read in the Gospel that the child leaped for joy when Mary arrived with Jesus in her womb. Strange to say it was this unborn child who recognized Christ's presence and the reason for Christ's coming—to proclaim the good news to the poor.

MORE THAN JUST NUMBERS

What was the good news Christ came to announce?

God is love.

God loves each one of us.

God loves me.

God loves you.

God has made you and me for greater things: to love and to be loved. We are not just numbers in the world.

That's why it is so beautiful to recognize the presence of unborn children as gifts from God. A child is the greatest of God's gifts to a family, because it is the fruit of the parents' love.

It is so wonderful to think that God has created that child! To think also that God has created you and me—that poor person in the street, that hungry person, and that ragged person. He has created us all in his image, for love.

We read something very beautiful in Scripture, where God assures us, "Even if a mother could forget her child, I will not forget you. I have carved you in the palm of my hand. I have called you by name" (Is 49:15-16).

Yet today we look over the world and see that little unborn children have become the target for death and destruction.[1] They are being destroyed and exterminated!

The terrible part is their own mothers decide to have them destroyed!

It is impossible for a mother to forget. But "even if a mother could forget, I will not forget you," says God. And yet today mothers forget their children!

Not only do they forget them, but they seek to have them destroyed.

Why?

Mothers are afraid their little unborn children will become a burden, the most beautiful creations of God's love.

We should thank God that our parents loved us, that our parents wanted us! Thank God!

Just imagine, if my mother hadn't wanted me, you would not have Mother Teresa. I would not have this opportunity to share with you if my mother had had me destroyed.

My mother loved me so much that later, when I grew up, she joyfully offered me to God. The gift he gave to her was the gift she gave back to him. And so, I am able to be with you and thank God with you.

I also want to thank God for all mothers who have wanted children and have decided to care for them.

Let us pray that every mother will want her child, that no mother will seek out ways of destroying her child, that no mother will feel she does not want her unborn child, that no mother will think of feeding and caring for one more child as a burden, but will instead recognize her child as a great gift from God.

The other day I was talking to a woman who had had an abortion eight years ago. What do you think she told me?

"Mother, I feel a pain in my heart whenever I see a child. When I see a child who is eight years old, I always think of my child who would be eight years old. It is an awful pain in my heart, believe me."

She was a Hindu, with a different degree of sensitivity to the value of human life, but Christian or non-Christian, that mother's love, that mother's pain, is there. Right up to the end of her life she will know, "I have killed my child, I decided to have my child destroyed!"

THE DESTROYER OF PEACE

Abortion is the great destroyer of peace in the world today. If a mother can kill her own child, what is left to prevent us from killing each other? There is nothing to prevent it.

What can we do? If necessary, let us start homes where we can gather together these children. Maybe they are not wanted, or maybe their parents cannot afford to take care of them. Let us then decide to take care of them ourselves.

By doing so, you and I will do something beautiful for God. We will give a wonderful home to children who would otherwise be destroyed and unwanted. We will fill those mothers' hearts with joy. Because, deep down in their hearts, they feel so sad.

What about your own family? Pray that God will come into your family, that your daughter or your son will be offered to God, dedicated to his service. Pray for your children:

To become his love, his compassion.
To become the reflection of his life in the world.
To become the hope of happiness in the world.
To become that burning flame of God in the world of today.

The world has never had such a great need for God's love as it does today.

It doesn't matter who you are. You may be a Protestant family or a Catholic family. Every family needs to pray, needs to turn to God, to believe in God and in his love.

When you feel disturbed or confused, when you are tempted to do something evil, when—if you are a mother—you are tempted to have your child destroyed, pray to God, "Help me now! Protect me from this sinful deed!" He will be there to give you the help to do his will.

Let us pray together, "Dear God, bless our families. Keep our families united." The family that prays together, stays together. And if we stay together, we will love one another. If we have prayer in our lives, there will be no cause for fear. Then the very love of Christ will penetrate and strengthen each of us.

RECEIVE HIM AND LIVE

Jesus loves you.

Jesus loves me.

Jesus loves those unborn children.

How do we know that Jesus loves us? By just looking at the cross!

The hands are still extended to embrace us.

The head is still bent to kiss us.

The heart is still open to receive us.

Are we there with him today?

Jesus is the same yesterday, today, and tomorrow. He stays there to make us understand that he wants us to love as he loves.

Will we love that unborn child?

Jesus has made himself the Bread of Life to satisfy our hunger for God. And he says, "Unless you eat my flesh and drink my blood, you cannot live."

We need Jesus in the Holy Eucharist.

He has made himself the Bread of Life—so fragile!—just so that you and I can receive him. He is so small like the image of a little, unborn child—so defenseless!—all so that you and I may receive him and live.

As the carrier of Jesus, let us ask Our Lady to come into our homes.

Let us ask her to help us make our families other Nazareths where joy, peace, love, and unity reign.

TEN

Carrying God's Love to Others

WE ALWAYS TALK ABOUT our love for God. I want to talk about his love for us.[1]

We can begin by reading in Scripture about his tender love for us. "Even if a mother could forget her child, I will not forget you. I have carved you on the palm of my hand" (Is 49:15-16).

Therefore, every time God looks at his hand, he sees me there. He sees you there too. It is something very beautiful to remember in times of suffering, loneliness, humiliation, and failure.

Remember, you are there in his hand.

You are precious to him.

He loves you.

What a truly wonderful thing!

GOD'S FORGIVING LOVE

The other day, a man, a journalist, asked me a strange question. He asked me, "Even you, do you have to go to confession?"

I said, "Yes, I go to confession every week."

And he said, "Then God must be very demanding if you all have to go to confession."

And I said, "Your own child sometimes does something wrong. What happens when your child comes to you and says, 'Daddy, I'm sorry?' What do you do?

"You put both of your arms around your child and kiss him. Why? Because that's your way of telling him that you love him.

"God does the same thing. He loves you tenderly."

Even when we sin or make a mistake, let's allow that to help us grow closer to God. Let's tell him humbly, "I know I shouldn't have done this, but even this failure I offer to you."

Let us ask our Lord to be with us in our moments of temptation. Just as Jesus was tempted, the devil will also tempt us.

We must not be afraid, because God loves us and will not fail to help us.

If we have sinned or made a mistake, let us go to him and say, "I'm sorry! I repent." God is a forgiving Father. His mercy is greater than our sins. He will forgive us.

This is humility: to have the courage to accept such humiliation and receive God's forgiveness.

We read in Scripture how Jesus came to proclaim the good news that God loves us.

He wants us today to be that love.

A co-worker of the Missionaries of Charity[2] is a carrier, a reflection of God's love. All of us must fill our hearts with determination to carry his love everywhere.

Why?

Because Jesus said, "You did it to me. I was hungry, naked, homeless, and lonely. And you did it to me."

That's why the Missionaries of Charity, as well as our co-workers who serve the sick, working people, contemplatives, youth, and co-workers who are priests and doctors, are all called to be carriers of God's love.

If in your family, your young daughter or son has done something wrong, forgive them. Show them the forgiving heart of God.

If we have trouble in families today, it is because children are lost. It is necessary for us to pray and then, with Our Lady, go out and look for the children to bring them home.

I had a very sad experience in England. One night, I saw a very young boy in the street. I said, "You should be at home with your parents."

And what did the little boy say? "My mother has thrown me out of the house because I have long hair!"

Love your children.

Love your husbands.

Love your wives.

Love them!

SHARE THE JOY OF LOVING

What does it mean to be a co-worker with the Missionaries of Charity? A co-worker is a person or a family where there is love, peace, and joy. If you have no peace and love in your own family or in your own heart, then how can you give it to others?

Love, to be true, has to hurt. I hope you will learn that in your lives and share the joy of loving, because a co-worker is someone who loves God. If you love God, then you will love those around you. Then there will be joy, love, and peace in your families. Then you will become carriers of God's love.

We will be very blessed to have the joy this love brings of working together and making our work a prayer.

With Jesus, for Jesus, to Jesus.

With God, for God, to God.

That way we are praying to God, not just doing our work.

When you are cooking, washing clothes, working hard in the office, do it all with joy. That will be your love for God in action!

ELEVEN

Love Changes Hearts

THE VOCATION OF OUR LADY was to accept Jesus into her life. She accepted being the hand-maid of the Lord. Then, in haste, she went to give Jesus to St. John the Baptist and his mother.

Today the same living Jesus comes to us and we too, like Mary, must go in haste to give him to others.

He made himself the hungry one, the naked one, the homeless one that we may be able to satisfy his love for us. He keeps saying, "You did it to me."

That call is directed to you.

Are you willing to answer?

It is for every Christian soul.

All of us are called to belong to God. But some of you are called in a special way to the priest-hood and the religious life. That vocation is to belong to Jesus so totally that nothing will separate you from the love of Christ.

And the work that you or I have to do is simply to put our love for Christ into living action.

BEING ONE WITH THE POOR

Our Sisters and our Brothers are called *Missionaries of Charity.* They are young people who are called to be the carriers of God's love.

In Yemen, where we were asked to go after six hundred years of no Christian presence, the presence of the Sisters has lit a new light in the lives of the people.

The Muslim governor wrote to Rome, "What are the Sisters doing here? They are just feeding the hungry Christ, clothing the naked Christ, giving a home to the homeless Christ."

When we arrived, we were put in charge of caring for the lepers. When I smelled the stench and saw the neglect of their bodies, I cried, "Jesus, how is it possible to leave you so neglected and foul-smelling?"

How is it possible to serve in such conditions? In order to achieve our work, we the

Missionaries of Charity, commit ourselves to love Christ with undivided love in chastity, through the freedom of poverty, in total surrender to obedience.[1]

But in our congregation we have a fourth vow: to give wholehearted, free service to the poorest of the poor. This vow, the vow of love, binds us totally to the poorest of the poor, and makes us fully and totally dependent on divine Providence.

THE EUCHARIST AND THE POOR

Someone could ask, "Who are the poorest of the poor?"

They are the unwanted, the unloved, the uncared for, the hungry, the forgotten, the naked, the homeless, the lepers, the alcoholics. But also we Missionaries of Charity are the poorest of the poor.

To be able to do what we do, and live the kind of life we live, every Missionary of Charity has to have her life united with the Eucharist. In the Eucharist, we see Christ in the appearance of bread. Then in the poor, we see Christ in a distressing disguise. The Eucharist and the poor are but one love.

To be able to work, to be able to see, to be able to love, we need this Eucharistic union.

Some years have gone by but I will never forget a young French girl who came to Calcutta one day.

She looked so worried. She went to work in our home for dying destitutes. Then, after ten days, she came to see me.

She hugged me and said, "I've found Jesus!"

I asked where she found Jesus.

"In the Home for Dying Destitutes," she answered.

"And what did you do after you found him?"

"I went to confession and Holy Communion after fifteen years."

Then I said again, "What else did you do?"

"I sent my parents a telegram saying that I found Jesus."

I looked at her and I said, "Now, pack up and go home. Go home and give joy, love, and peace to your parents."

She went home radiating joy, because her heart was filled with joy. She went home, and what joy she brought to her family!

Why?

Because she had lost the innocence of her youth and had gotten it back again.

CHANGED BY LOVE

The Sisters take care of thousands and thousands of lepers. Our Sisters wash lepers covered with wounds, for they are the wounds of Jesus. It is there that we find Jesus.

One day, one of our Sisters was lovingly washing a leper's open sores. A Muslim cleric was standing by and watching. He said, "All these years I have believed that Jesus Christ was a prophet. Today I believe that Jesus Christ is God if he is able to give such joy to this Sister to do this work with so much love."

In New York, we have a home for AIDS patients, who are dying from what I call "the leprosy of the West." On Christmas Eve, I opened this house as a gift to Jesus for his birthday. We started with fifteen beds for some poor AIDS patients and for four young men I brought out of jail because they didn't want to die there. They were our first guests.

I had made a little chapel for them. There these young people, who had not been near Jesus, or used to praying or confession, could come back to him if they wanted to. Thanks to God's blessing and his love, their hearts completely changed.

Once when I went there, one of them had to

go to the hospital. He said to me, "Mother Teresa, you are my friend. I want to speak to you alone." So the Sisters went out, and he spoke.

And what did this man say? This was someone who hadn't been to confession or received Holy Communion in twenty-five years. In all those years, he had had nothing to do with Jesus.

He told me, "You know, Mother Teresa, when I get a terrible headache, I compare it with the pain that Jesus had when they crowned him with thorns. When I get that terrible pain in my back, I compare it with Jesus when he was scourged. When I get that terrible pain in my hands and feet, I compare it with the pain Jesus had when they crucified him. I ask you to take me back home. I want to die with you."

I got permission from the doctor to take him back home with me. I took him to the chapel.

I have never seen anybody talk to God the way that young man talked to him. There was such an understanding love between Jesus and him. After three days, he died.

It is hard to understand the change that young man experienced. What brought it about? It was probably the tender love the

Sisters gave him that made him understand God loved him.

In Calcutta alone, we have picked up thirty-six thousand people in twenty-five years, around seventeen thousand of whom have died a most beautiful death. I feel that the greatest dignity for a human life is to die in peace with God.

One day I picked up a man from the gutter. His body was covered with worms.

I brought him to our house, and what did this man say?

He did not curse. He did not blame anyone. He just said, "I've lived like an animal in the street, but I'm going to die like an angel, loved and cared for!"

It took us three hours to clean him. Finally, the man looked up at the Sister and said, "Sister, I'm going home to God." And then he died.

I've never seen such a radiant smile on a human face as the one I saw on that man's face.

He went home to God.

See what love can do!

It is possible that young Sister did not think about it at the moment, but she was touching the body of Christ. Jesus said so when he said,

"Whatever you did to the least of my brethren, you did to me" (Mt 25:40).

And this is where you and I fit into God's plan.

He has kindled his love in our hearts, so that we may love those we meet with his love.

TWELVE

The Hands and Feet of Jesus

JESUS SPENT MOST of his time repeating on earth one thing, "Love one another as God loves you. As the Father has loved me, I love you. Love one another" (Jn 15:9).

When we look at the cross, we discover[1] how much Jesus loved us. When we look at the tabernacle, we know how much he loves us now. That is why it is very important for us, if we really want to love and to be loved, to learn to pray. Let us teach our children to pray. Let's pray with them.

Think of the fruit of our prayer:

The fruit of prayer is faith. Prayer leads us to say: "I believe."
the fruit of faith is love. Faith leads us to say: "I love."

The fruit of love is service. Love leads us to say, "I want to serve."
And the fruit of service is peace.

LOVE AND SERVICE BEGIN AT HOME

We should never forget: love begins at home. Yes today, we are having a terrible time, because we have so many broken, unhappy families.

They don't pray together. There is no sharing. There is no joy of serving each other.

Poverty is not the cause.

No, it is not poverty.

What then is causing this?

It is unbridled ambition for things and for status, something that interferes in our lives, that we love more than our family.

That's why I very often tell young people, "It is very beautiful for a young man to love a young woman. And for a young woman to love a young man. But make sure you love each other with a pure heart, with a clean heart— more than money, more than any possession. The greatest gift you can give to each other is a clean heart and a virgin body." The loss of purity, of chastity, of virginity has affected so many lives.

I never tire of talking about family life and of expressing my desire for families to be holy and united, where love reigns among all family members.

How will husband and wife stay together? We have the marvelous example of the Holy Family of Nazareth in plain view.

Why do we call them the "Holy Family of Nazareth"? Because there was such living holiness among them. They were of one heart, full of love, in the very heart of God.

There was no division.

There was no misunderstanding.

We know how much St. Joseph loved Mary. When he found out that she was with child, he could have presumed the worst. He could have gone straight to the chief priest to denounce her for adultery. But no, he did not do it, because he loved her so tenderly! He would have preferred to be stoned rather than have Mary stoned. Here we have an example of tender love, of mutual concern. And an angel told St. Joseph in a dream that this child was God's very own.

If father and mother have that concern for each other, naturally, the children will learn from them. And when the time comes for them to be parents, they will know what to do and how to do it.

Teach your children to love one another.

Teach your children to have respect for each other.

Teach your children to share.

Teach your children, because nowadays, many schools do not teach these things.

I will never forget how a little four-year-old Hindu child taught me how to show great love.

It was a time when we had no sugar in Calcutta. I do not know how that little one heard that Mother Teresa had no sugar for her children. He went home to his parents and told them, "I will not eat sugar for three days. I'll give my sugar to Mother Teresa."

That little one loved with great love. He loved until it hurt. And so must we.

Children and young people have generous hearts. They are eager to help. One day two young people came to our house and gave me a large amount of money.

"Where did you get so much money?" I asked them.

They said, "Two days ago, we got married. And before getting married, we decided not to have a wedding feast, not to buy wedding clothes, so we could give you the money."

I know very well what a big sacrifice that means to a Hindu family. So, I asked them, "Why did you do that?"

And you know what answer they gave me?

"We love each other so much that we wanted to share the joy of loving with the people you serve."

They wanted to share the joy of loving.

Do you know that right where you live, there are many people in the streets? Hundreds come every day to our places, just for a little food, a little human warmth, a smile, a handshake—nothing more.

Do you know that?

Come and see!

I will never forget one day in Venezuela when I went to visit a family who had given us a lamb. I went to thank them and there I found out that they had a badly crippled child. I asked the mother, "What is the child's name? What do you call him at home?"

The mother gave me a most beautiful answer. "We call him 'Teacher of Love,' because he keeps on teaching us how to love. Everything we do for him is our love for God in action."

What a beautiful spirit!

LIGHTING ONE LAMP

I had another beautiful experience when we opened our house in Melbourne, Australia. The Sisters and I divided up and went around to the poor, the "skid row" area where we had our house.

I went to one of the small houses that was made out of refuse, and I found there an old man neglected and surrounded by filth. You can just imagine what it was like!

I said to him, "Please allow me to clean your place, wash your clothes, and make your bed."

He said, "Don't bother. I'm all right."

I said, "You'll feel better if you allow me to clean everything up a bit."

"Well, you can if you want," he answered.

And I cleaned and washed everything. Then in the corner of the room, I saw a beautiful lamp, covered with filth.

I asked him, "Do you light this lamp in the evening?"

He looked at me and said, "For whom? For years and years, nobody has come to see me."

"Would you light the lamp if my Sisters came to see you?" I asked.

"Yes, of course!" he said with a smile.

I cleaned the lamp and left it sparkling. The Sisters started going there every evening and he lit the lamp for them.

I forgot completely about him. After two years, he sent word to me through the Sisters in Australia, "Tell my friend the light she has lit in my life is still burning. It is still burning!''

One day, we picked up a man off the street who looked like a fairly well-to-do person. He was completely drunk. He couldn't even stand up because he was so drunk!

We took him to our home. The Sisters treated him with such love, such care, such kindness.

After a fortnight, he told the Sisters, "Sisters, my heart is open. Through you I have come to realize that God loves me. I've felt his tender love for me. I want to go home." And we helped him get ready to go home.

After a month, he came back to our home and gave the Sisters his first paycheck. He told the Sisters, "Do to others what you have done to me." And he walked away a different person.

Love had brought him back to his family, to his children's tenderness, to his wife's understanding love.

Let us ask Our Lady to teach us how to love and how to have the courage to share.

LEARN TO SHARE

Some time ago I made a trip to Ethiopia. Our Sisters were working there during that terrible drought. Just as I was about to leave for

Ethiopia, I found myself surrounded by many children.

Each one of them gave something, "Take this to the children! Take this to the children!" they would say. They had many gifts that they wanted to give to our poor.

Then a small child, who for the first time had a piece of chocolate, came up to me and said, "I do not want to eat it. You take it and give it to the children."

This little one gave a great deal, because he gave it all, and he gave something that was very precious to him.

Have you ever experienced the joy of giving? I do not want you to give me from your abundance. I never allow people to have fund-raisers for me. I don't want that. I want you to give of yourself.

The love you put into the giving is the most important thing. If you want a happy family, if you want a holy family, learn to share. Give your hands to serve and your hearts to love.

THIRTEEN

God Loves Children

L ET US ASK MARY to be a mother to us. Since she was Jesus' mother, she taught Jesus how to live family life beautifully in Nazareth.

I am very happy to be surrounded by children,[1] because Jesus had a very special love for children. Many children came to see Jesus, and the apostles said to them, "Don't come!" But Jesus said, "Let the children come to me. I love them."

I say to children: you know God loves you very much! That is why he sent Jesus to come among us. And Jesus said again and again, "Love one another as I have loved you!" (Jn 15:12). Jesus loved you so much that he died on the cross for us.

Because he wants to remain with us, he is present in the Blessed Sacrament. Most of you have received Jesus.

You remember why he comes to your hearts. Because he loves you so much.

EVERYDAY CLOTHES FOR FIRST COMMUNION

We have, in India, as in many other places, many poor children in our homes. Many of them have no one to love them. That is why you must thank God for giving you such wonderful parents who love you so much.

But I assure you that those little children are very beautiful children. I have a wonderful letter from a little girl. She said that she was going to make her first Holy Communion.

She told her parents, "Don't buy First Communion clothes for me. I will make my First Communion with everyday clothes. Give me the money and I will send it to Mother Teresa for her poor children."

You must have heard what terrible things happened in Ethiopia, where many children died of hunger because of the terrible drought. Our Sisters are in Ethiopia taking care of many people, including children.

When the children from other countries heard that I was going to Ethiopia, many little children came to me and gave me all kinds of little gifts and some money.

One little boy had received a piece of chocolate from somebody for the first time. He came to me and said, "Mother Teresa, please give this chocolate to some child in Ethiopia." This is the beautiful love of a child like you!

I want you to pray together with me for all the poor children in the world. Let us pray that they too, like you and I, have a chance to be loved and to love.

I will pray for you that one day Jesus will speak to you, to invite you to give your hearts, your minds, your bodies, and your souls to God. I will pray that you will say yes to him.

I hope there is among you some little girl who will become a Missionary of Charity. (And why not? Also some little boy who will become a Brother Missionary of Charity.)

I hope you will be the peace, joy, and love of Christ in many mission countries.

I ask only one thing of you: Ask Our Lady for help. Ask her to keep your hearts always clean, because a clean heart can see Jesus.

Jesus said, "Whatever you do for the least of my brethren, such as giving him a glass of water in my name, you do it to me" (Mt 25:40). You see how wonderful it is: whenever we do little things for our brothers and sisters in our own families, we do it for Jesus.

Ask your father and mother to teach you how to pray. The fruit of prayer is love, and the fruit of love is sharing the joy of loving.

I ask you to pray for us also. God bless you!.

FOURTEEN

Loving People, Not Things

FOR SOME TIME NOW, we have had a small community of Sisters in Guatemala. We came there during the earthquake of 1972 which caused so much damage.

The Sisters in Guatemala came to love and serve as they do everywhere. They told me something beautiful about a very poor man who was picked up from the city streets and brought to one of our homes. He was very sick, disabled, hungry, helpless. But somehow, with the help of everybody, he got well again.

He told the Sisters, "I want to go and leave this bed for somebody else who may need it as much as I needed it when I came here."

And I believe now he has a job. I don't think he earns much, but he is working. Every time he gets a little money, he remembers the other disabled people who are in the home and comes to see them.

He always brings something for them.

Even with the little he has, he always brings something.

This is the great gift of our poor people: the love they have.

SOMEONE OR SOMETHING TO LOVE

I will tell you another good example of how generous and great our people are.

We had picked up a young orphan boy whose mother had died in the Home for Dying Destitutes. She had come from a good family, but had come down in life because of difficult circumstances.

The boy grew up and wanted to become a priest. When he was asked, "Why do you want to become a priest?" he gave a very simple answer. "I want to do for other children what Mother Teresa has done for me. I want to love as she loved me. I want to serve as she served me."

Today he is a priest, devoted to loving all those who have nothing and no one—those who have forgotten what human love is, or the warmth of a human touch, or even the kindness of a smile.

I cannot remember now in what city I was, but I do remember that I did not see any children on the street. I missed the children very badly. While I was walking down the street, suddenly I saw a baby carriage. A young woman was pushing the carriage, and I crossed the street just to see the child.

To my terrible surprise, there was no child in the carriage. There was a little dog!

Apparently the hunger in the heart of that woman had to be satisfied. So, not having a child, she looked for a substitute. She found a dog.

In many places, children are neglected, but animals are cared for and pampered. Animals are given special food and special things. I love dogs myself very much, but still I cannot bear seeing a dog given the place of a child.

I must tell you something that was a surprise for me and may be a surprise for you.

We deal with thousands and thousands of very poor people in Calcutta. As you may know, there are over ten million people in that city, but up to now I am not aware of one woman among the very poor who has had an abortion.

I do not know such a woman who has had an abortion.

All of them have given birth to their children.

At times they might put their children in the garbage, hoping that someone will take care of them. But I know of not one who has decided to destroy her child. A mother's love should never allow her to destroy her own children.

THE BABIES OF OUR LEPER PEOPLE

We care for more than fifty-three thousand leprosy patients. With the help of the Indian government, we are creating rehabilitation centers for them.

As you know, in the time of Jesus, lepers were not accepted by anybody. They had to hide in cemeteries, stay away from everybody, and ring a bell as they were passing by to give people a chance to move away from them.

Today love for Jesus is allowing more and more people to approach lepers. The number of those who feel like helping them keeps growing. More and more lepers are beginning to realize there are people who love them, who do not mind being near them. Quite the contrary!

In our leprosy centers, we are also building children's homes. The miracle of God is that children born of leprosy patients are perfectly clean and healthy at birth.

Before the children are born, we prepare the parents to give them up for the sake of their children's future. They must give them up right away, before they start feeding their children, before they even kiss them. Our Sisters care for the children in the home attached to the rehabilitation center.

One day, I saw a mother and father put their baby between them. It was a newborn baby boy, three days old.

They put the baby between them, and each one looked at the little one. They extended their hands towards the child, and then they would pull back. They made gestures, wanting to kiss their child, and again they would pull back.

I cannot forget the deep love that father and mother had for their little child. I picked up the child, and I could see the father and mother following him with their eyes as I walked away. I held up the child towards them, and they kept on looking and looking at him with great tenderness until I disappeared from their sight.

What agony and sorrow it caused them! They are allowed to see their child, but they cannot touch him. It hurt them to give up their child. But because they loved him more than they loved themselves, they had the strength to give him up.

It is beautiful to see the enormous sacrifice our leper parents make for the sake of their children, so that they will not be infected and may grow up as normal, happy children.

"IT MUST BE POSSIBLE!"

In Calcutta, every night we send word to all the clinics, police stations, and hospitals, "Please do not destroy the children. I will take the children." So our home is always very full of children.

There is a joke in Calcutta, "Mother Teresa is always talking about abortion and about family planning, but she certainly has not practiced this at all. Every day she has more and more children!"

We have many children in our homes for unwed mothers; one hundred and seventy babies are born every day. Can you imagine that?

Yet God has worked a miracle. Even in India, every day we have one or two families who come to adopt a child. Many come from abroad, but many children are being adopted in India.

You may not understand this great miracle, but for us who live in India, who work among

Indians, this is the greatest miracle that could happen. According to the caste system, my children and myself and all the Sisters are untouchables. Therefore, to take one of our children into a family is something unbelievable. It goes against the whole cultural and religious life of the nation.

Nevertheless, Indian parents are really taking our children in. According to Hindu law, an adopted child becomes like flesh and blood of the family that adopts him.

This does not happen in any other country with such a caste system except India. So this is one of those greatest miracles that God has worked.

I remember when I told Mrs. Indira Gandhi, the former prime minister of India, what I was doing with the children. She said, "No, that is not possible!"

I said to her, "But we are doing it. It must be possible!"

We have a lot to learn from our poor people. We receive much more from them than what we give to them.

FIFTEEN

Faith Is a Gift of God

THE PRESENCE OF CHRIST always creates love to give, because that is what Jesus learned from his Father. When we are given such love to share, God is telling us, "Now, leave immediately. Go in haste, not slowly."

Very often, people laugh at me, because I am in such a hurry to share Jesus' love. I say to them, "Our Lady always seemed to be in a hurry for such a reason." When you want to catch Jesus and share him, you must always be in a hurry.

You know the story of the man in the Gospel (Zaccheus, Lk 19:1-10). He thought he was such a big man, so big that he could not see Jesus.

One day he realized that he was so small. It was the desire to see Jesus that made him realize that he was small.

What did he do?

What would a child have done?

He climbed the tree.

He made himself a child, he acted like a child.

What did Jesus do?

He left everybody, came near the tree, and said, "Come down! Come quickly, Zaccheus. I am going to your house."

That word "haste" has a wonderful meaning for each one of us, when we receive Jesus in Holy Communion. The urgent longing to give him to others should fill us. It should fill us with an intimate, deep love for Christ.

FAITH IS A GIFT

In India, I was asked by some government people, "Don't you want to make us all Christians?"

I said, "Naturally, I would like to give the treasure I have to you, but I cannot. I can only pray for you to have the courage to receive it."

Faith is a gift from God.

I remember that one day I picked up a man from the gutter. Except for his face, his whole body was covered with wounds. I brought him to our home. (We have a home right next to the temple of Kali, the Hindu goddess of fear and destruction.)

What did this man say? "I have lived like an animal in the street, but I am going to die like an angel, loved and cared for."

After three hours (we just had time to give him a bath, to clean him and put him in bed), he died with a big smile on his face. The priest gave him a special blessing, asking that his sins would be forgiven, so that he could see the face of God for all eternity. And I believe that he received that gift.

There was no complaint, there was no cursing, there was no fear . . . he died in peace.

There is a natural conscience in every human being to know right from wrong. I deal with thousands who are non-Christians, and you can see such a conscience at work in their lives, drawing them to God.

In everybody there is a tremendous hunger for God, in spite of all appearances.

A FLAME THAT CONSUMES

The words of Jesus, *"Love one another as I have loved you,"* (Jn 15:12) must be not only a light for us but a flame that consumes the self in us.

Love, in order to survive, must be nourished by sacrifices, especially the sacrifice of self.

People are trying to make God a relic from the past. But you, by your love, by the purity of your lives and your compassion, can prove to the world that God is up-to-date.

The co-workers of Christ must give special attention to those who feel unwanted and deprived of love.

For the worst disease of all is feeling unloved. The greatest sin is the terrible indifference to those on the fringe of the social system.

May the sick and suffering find in us angels of comfort and consolation. May the poor by seeing us be drawn to Christ and invite him into their lives.

SIXTEEN

Our Masters, the Poor

OUR BEAUTIFUL WORK with and for the poor is a privilege and a gift for us. St. Vincent de Paul used to tell the young aspirants to his order, "Remember, the poor are our masters. We must love and obey them."

I think that if we go to the poor with that love, with only the desire to give God to them, to bring the joy of Christ (which is our strength) into their homes; if they look at us and see Jesus and his love and compassion in us—I think the world will soon be full of peace and love.

SISTERS OF FIFTEEN CONGREGATIONS

Quite a few years ago, when there were refugees from Bangladesh in India, the Indian government allowed religious women from all over the world to come and help us in our work of serving the refugees. Those Sisters were from fifteen different orders.

Our little order, being so young and small, was like a drop of water in the big ocean of these older, bigger orders. And yet each of these Sisters refused to go live somewhere else with the other congregations. They all wanted to share a life of poverty and prayer with the Missionaries of Charity.

They wanted to know what poverty is, to be able to know the poor, love them, and serve them. And so they lived with us for six months.

Finally, when they were leaving, each one in her own way expressed her gratitude by saying, "I have received much more than I have given and I will never be the same person."

I hear that those very Sisters have gone back to their congregations. And now in their own way, they are more sensitive to people who are unwanted, unloved, and uncared for.

POOR PEOPLE DO NOT COMPLAIN

Our Sisters and Brothers work for the poorest of the poor—the sick, the dying, the lepers, the abandoned children. But I can tell you that in all these years I have never heard the poor grumble or curse, nor have I seen any of them dejected with sadness. The poor are great people, they can accept very difficult things.

We have so many lepers to look after. When we ask for volunteers among our young Sisters to go and work with the lepers, every hand is raised.

Even though they are so disfigured and so difficult to look at, here is Christ in our midst. For he had said, "I was sick and hungry and naked and homeless. And you did it to me." And, like Christ, they do not complain.

Jesus cannot deceive us. Each time you make these sacrifices, each time you think of the poor both near and far off, every time you give up something you would like and give it to the poor, you are feeding the hungry Christ, you are clothing the naked Christ, you are giving a home to the homeless Christ.

Whether you are directly serving the poor or not, whenever you think of the poor and make sacrifices for them, you are really doing it to Christ.

SEVENTEEN

Loving God in Our Neighbors

JESUS WAS SENT to bring us the good news that God is love, that he loves us. He wants us to love one another as he loves us.

Jesus was born into a family and stayed in Nazareth for thirty years.

He had come to redeem the world, yet he spent thirty years in Nazareth, doing the humble work of an ordinary person.

People often used to say, "But he is the son of Joseph! How could he do this . . . ? He is the son of Mary, we know him. . . ."

He spent all those years just living out family life.

They must have prayed together.

They must have worked together.

They must have loved each other.

Yes, that was true family life.

There was peace!
There was unity!
There was joy!
Bring prayer back into your family life, and you too will see that unity, the bond of joyful love that will bind you together. Maybe there is poverty and suffering in your families. But sharing together, loving together will help you.

THE RUNAWAY CHILD

One day I found a little girl in the street, so I took her to our children's home. We have a nice place and good food there. We gave her clean clothes and we made her as happy as we could.

After a few hours, the little girl ran away. I looked for her, but I couldn't find her anywhere. Then after a few days, I found her again.

And, again, I brought her to our home and told a Sister, "Sister, please, follow this child wherever she goes."

The little girl ran away again. But the Sister followed to find out where she was going and why she kept running away.

She followed the little girl and discovered that the little one's mother was living under a tree in the street. The mother had placed two stones there and did her cooking under that tree.

The Sister sent word to me and I went there. I found joy on that little girl's face, because she was with her mother who loved her and was making special food for her in that little open place.

I asked the little girl, "How is it that you would not stay with us? You had so many beautiful things in our home."

She answered, "I could not live without my mother. She loves me." That little girl was happier to have the meager food her mother was cooking in the street than all the things I had given her.

While the child was with us, I could scarcely see a smile on her face. But when I found her there with her mother, in the street, they were smiling.

Why?

Because they were family.

The father must have gone to collect whatever had been thrown away, I suppose.

That little one could do without many things, but she could not do without the love of her family, of her mother. Unhappiness does not necessarily come from not having this or that. If we have each other, we have everything.

This is why it is very important for mothers and fathers to love their children.

Children will remain faithful.

Children will love their families.

Children who are loved never run away from home.

No young man, no young woman, runs away from home because they do not have this or that. They only run away from a home where love is missing.

"I CANNOT DIE"

Some of those young people who ran away have gotten sick with the disease called AIDS. Maybe you have never experienced that. It is something very terrible.

We have opened a home in New York for AIDS patients, who find themselves among the most unwanted people of today.

What a tremendous change has been brought about in their lives just because of a few Sisters who take care of them, and have made a home for them!

A home of love!

A gift of love!

A place, perhaps the only place, where they feel loved, where they are somebody to someone. This has changed their lives in such a way that they die a most beautiful death. Not one of them has yet died in distress.

The other day, a Sister called to tell me that one of the young men (all are young people) was dying. But, strange to say, he couldn't die.

So she asked him, "What is it?" (He was struggling with death!) "What is wrong?"

And he said, "Sister, I cannot die until I ask my father to forgive me."

So the Sister found out where the father was, and she called him. And something extraordinary happened, like a living page from the Gospel: The father embraced his son and cried, "My son! My beloved son!"

And the son begged the father, "Forgive me! Forgive me!"

And the two of them clinged to each other tenderly.

Two hours later the young man died.

WHAT LOVE CAN DO

See what love can do! It is something that can help us to open our hearts to God.

In the world today we have so much suffering, so much killing, so much sorrow, because people have lost the joy of loving God in their hearts. With that gone, they cannot share the joy of loving each other.

One day I was walking down the street in London. And I saw a tall, thin man on the corner, all huddled up looking most miserable.

I went up to him, shook his hand, and asked him how he was. Then he looked up at me and said, "Oh! After such a long, long, long time I feel the warmth of a human hand!" And he sat up.

There was such a beautiful smile on his face, because somebody was kind to him. Just shaking his hand had made him feel like somebody.

For me, he was Jesus in a distressing disguise. I gave him the joy of being loved, the feeling of being loved by somebody.

Somebody loves us, too—God himself. Truly, the tenderness of God's love is most extraordinary. When we look at the cross, we know how much Jesus loved us *then*. When we look at the tabernacle, we know how much he loves us *now*.

That's why you should ask your parish priests to give you the joy of having adoration of the Blessed Sacrament at least once a week.

Be alone with Jesus.

Then your hearts will feel the joy that only he can give.

I will give you one more beautiful example of God's love. A man came to our house and said, "My only child is dying! The doctor has prescribed a medicine that you can get only in England." (Now I have permission from our government to store life-saving medicines that are gathered from all over the country. We have many people that go from house to house and gather leftover medicines. And they bring them to us and we give them to our poor people. We have thousands of people who come to our dispensaries.) While we were talking, a man came in with a basket of medicines.

I looked at that basket of medicines: right on the top was the very medicine that man needed for his dying child! If it had been underneath, I wouldn't have seen it.

If he had come earlier or later, I would not have remembered. He came just in time.

I stood in front of that basket and I was thinking, "There are millions of children in the world, and God is concerned with that little child in the slums of Calcutta. To send that man at that very moment! To put the medicine right on the top, so I could see it!"

See God's tender concern for you and for me!
He would do the same thing for each one of you.

RELYING ON GOD IN OUR
THREE HUNDRED FIFTY-TWO HOUSES

We Missionaries of Charity take a special
vow to God to give whole-hearted, free service
to the poorest of the poor. We have no income,
no church assistance, no government salary, no
government grants. We have none of that.

And yet we deal with thousands and thousands and thousands of people, and we have
never had to say to anybody, "We're sorry, we
have run out of supplies."

The Sisters are now (September 1987) in three
hundred fifty-two houses, caring for the poorest of the poor: the unwanted, unloved, the
mentally retarded, the crippled, the abandoned,
and other people left alone with great sufferings. If you ever find somebody like that, the
Sisters are here. At any time, there is a home for
them.

You can also do your part. Small things—
even maybe a smile, maybe just helping a blind
person cross the street—become the works of
peace. A beggar one day came up to me and

said, "Mother Teresa, everybody gives you things for the poor. I also want to give you something. But today, I am only able to get ten pence. I want to give that to you."

I said to myself, "If I take it, he might have to go to bed without eating. If I don't take it, I will hurt him."

So I took it.

And I've never seen so much joy on anybody's face who has given his money or food, as I saw on that man's face. He was happy that he too could give something.

This is the joy of loving.

I will pray for you to experience the joy of loving, and that you will share this joy, first in your own families and then with all those you meet.

Also pray for us that we may continue doing God's work with great love, and that we don't spoil it.

EIGHTEEN

Seeing, Loving, and Serving Christ in the Poor

Q: Mother Teresa, do you find it easy to carry out your work among the poor?[1]

MT: Of course, it would not be easy without an intense life of prayer and a spirit of sacrifice. It wouldn't be easy either if we didn't see in the poor, Christ who continues to suffer the sorrows of his passion. At times, we would be happy if we could get the poor to live peacefully with each other. It is so hard for those who have been deprived of their basic needs to live in harmony and support their neighbors, and not see them as dangerous competitors, capable of making their state of misery even worse! That's why we cannot offer them anything but our testimony of love, seeing Christ himself in each one of them, no matter how repugnant they seem to us.

Q: How do you get so many vocations?

MT: God is the one who sends them. They come and see. Sometimes they come from very far away. Many of them first hear about us by what they read in the newspapers.

Q: With the Sisters you have available, do you accomplish all that you would like?

MT: Unfortunately, the needs are always greater than our ability to meet them.

Q: Mother Teresa, what moves you to continually open new homes?

MT: If God continues sending us so many vocations without fail, we believe that this is not so we can keep them hidden in convents. Rather God wants to multiply the work of helping the poorest of the poor.

Q: What criteria do you use for opening homes in India and abroad?

MT: We never open any home without already having been invited by the local bishop. In fact, the present requests for help far surpass our capability to meet them. As a general rule based on our constitution, when we receive an invitation to open a new home, we first go and investigate the living conditions of the poor in that area. We never decide to open a home for any other reason than that of serving the poor. Normally, the decision to start a new home follows these investigations, except in cases of the most extreme need.

Q: What importance do you give to outward appearances?

MT: Very little or none. As for our habit, even though the sari is part of our usual way of dressing, we would be willing to modify or relinquish it if we found out that we were not accepted for being dressed that way. We would adopt another form of dress if it were better accepted by the poor wherever we felt called to carry out our work.

Q: Do you find it easy to carry out your work?

MT: We are taught from the very first moment to discover Christ under the distressing disguise of the poor, the sick, the outcasts. Christ presents himself to us under every disguise: the dying, the paralytic, the leper, the invalid, the orphan. It is faith that makes our work, which demands both special preparation and a special calling, easy or at least more bearable. Without faith, our work could become an obstacle for our religious life since we come across blasphemy, wickedness, and atheism at every turn.

Q: In your work, how much importance do you give to religious matters?

MT: We are not simply social workers, but missionaries. Nevertheless, we try to do evangelization exclusively through our work, allowing God to manifest himself in it. We teach catechism to the children in our orphanages. We only take the initiative with adults when they ask for instruction or when they ask us questions about religious matters. All of the Sisters receive a good religious formation during their novitiate and more training in later years. We do not like to take the place of others who are more competent in some subjects than we are. For example, we refer more difficult questions to priests, besides those that are obviously related to their ministry. As for the criteria we use to determine our assistance, we never base our assistance on the religious beliefs of the needy but on the need itself. We are not concerned with the religious beliefs of those we help. We only focus on how urgent the need is.

Q: Do the Missionaries of Charity have any preferences among the people they assist?

MT: If there is any, it is for the poorest of the poor, the most abandoned, those who have no one to care for them, the orphans, the dying, the lepers.

Q: According to some, the work of the Missionaries of Charity in the Home for Dying Destitutes only prolongs the misery of those cared for. Those who are restored to health return to the streets where they will encounter the same problems of disease and misery. What is your response to this?

MT: Whenever it is possible we try not to limit our care to just medical attention. We try to achieve the human and social rehabilitation of those who are restored to health. It is true that in many cases those who recuperate prefer the freedom of the streets to the closed spaces of our surroundings, but this is something that we cannot prevent. We act under the conviction that every time we feed the poor, we are offering food to Christ himself. Whenever we clothe a naked human being, we are clothing Christ himself. Whenever we offer shelter to the dying, we are sheltering Christ himself.

Q: There are those who assert that the medical training of the Missionaries of Charity is too rudimentary for people who care for the seriously ill.

MT: I know that. Our medical training is limited, but we try to offer assistance and care to those who, in most cases, have no one to give them even the most basic medical care.

Q: It has also been said that the care that you give to such desperate cases could be better channeled to those who have a better chance of survival.

MT: We try to help all those who need care, but we give preference to those who have the greatest need of help. We do not turn our backs on anyone. No one is left out of our will to serve. In each suffering brother we see the likeness of Christ suffering in him. Even if we have to narrow our care down to a few, because of necessity or limited resources, our desire is to expand our charity.

Q: At times, there isn't much you do or can do for the dying, is there?

MT: We can, at least, leave them with the impression of something important: that there are people willing to truly love them, because the dying too are children of God and deserve to be loved as much or maybe even more than anyone else.

Q: Don't you ever experience repugnance in the face of so much misery?

MT: Yes, we carry out our work mainly among the dying, the destitute elderly, poor orphaned children, and lepers. We cannot deny that our work is hard for us in many cases. We don't always carry it out under acceptable conditions. But all of us are better off working among the poor than among the rich. This is our lifetime work. During the novitiate, which lasts two years, we dedicate half the day to carrying out our work among the poor. The novices work under the supervision of older Sisters. Then, before making our final vows, we spend several more years serving the poor. Our work becomes almost a habit for us, which makes it easier, instinctive, and natural, without being mechanical.

Q: What significance do you attribute to your mission of assistance?

MT: Our service is not limited to offering just material relief. We want to offer whatever is necessary so that the poorest of the poor don't feel abandoned, and so they realize that there are people who care about them. We want our work to accomplish what a high-level official in our country once said to the Sisters: "It is Christ who is again walking among us doing good in favor of men."

Q: What do you do for lepers?

MT: We offer assistance to more than twenty thousand afflicted with this disease, just in Calcutta alone, and to fifty thousand in all of India. We realize this is nothing in a country where there are four million victims of leprosy. The first thing we do for those who receive our help is to convince them that they really have this disease. We get the necessary medicines for them and we try to cure them. Today it is not necessary for lepers to live in isolation. If we can help them in time, they can be fully cured. So what the Sisters try to do first of all is to convince the people to confront this disease. In India, leprosy is considered a punishment from

God. It is part of the religion of the people. The Sisters try to do everything possible to cure them and rid them of this belief.

Q: How much do the medicines for each leper cost?

MT: Really, we don't pay for the medicines. They are given to us. We receive medicines from many places, starting with the United States, Germany, France, England, and Switzerland. In any case, they don't cost a lot. I don't have an exact idea of how much each patient's medicine costs.

Q: Do you receive enough to help the lepers?

MT: Yes, for the moment at least, as far as medicines are concerned. We also have to buy vitamin pills, analgesics, and some other health aids. Besides these things, of course, we need other aids like clothing, bandages, basic commodities, antiseptics, deodorizers, and lotions.

Q: From whom do you especially receive aid?

MT: From everyone, thanks be to God. We have Hindu, Muslim, Parsee, Jewish, Buddhist, Protestant, and naturally, Catholic co-workers and benefactors.

Q: Has it ever occurred to you that you could end up without resources for your works?

MT: We never have any surplus, but we have never lacked what we need. Sometimes it happens in strange ways, almost miraculously. We wake up without resources, with the anguish of not being able to tend to our needy. A few hours later, we almost always see the most unexpected provisions arrive from anonymous donors. From Catholics, Protestants, Buddhists, Jews, Parsees, Muslims, and Hindus. From adherents of any religion or of no religion. From the rich and from the poor.

Q: What is the work you accomplish like?

MT: It is not important work in and of itself, but the humblest that exists. We think that its value comes from the spirit of love for God that inspires it. It is impossible to love God without loving our neighbor. At the same time, no Missionary of Charity forgets the words of Christ: I was hungry and you gave me to eat. This is what we are trying to do: feed, clothe, and visit Christ in the sick, the dying, the lepers, and the abandoned children.

Q: Could you talk about your work with abandoned children?

MT: Yes, we started with them and we still are with them, even though they are not our only work. Orphans and abandoned children are unfortunately the kind of children that are never in short supply. Once in the first years of our work, a policeman brought us a group of children that were caught in the act of stealing. They were too young to send to jail with common criminals. I asked them why they had done it. They explained to me that every evening from five to eight o'clock adults gave them lessons on how to commit robberies.

Q: What kind of a future do the children you rescue have?

MT: I don't believe there is a better way of helping India than to prepare a better tomorrow for today's children. We take care of the poorest of those children, the ones that are picked up in the slums. Each one of them needs a monthly allowance of just a few dollars. It is very moving to see children from other countries—French, English, German, Spanish, Swiss, Danish, and Italian children—donate from their savings. We open a savings account for each child we take in. When the child is older and if he is capable, he receives higher education. We see that those children who do not have the aptitude for higher education receive an education in the trades, so that they will be able to make a living for themselves.

Q: You Missionaries of Charity witness terrible injustices. How do you react to them?

MT: The injustices are there for everyone to see. It is up to large organizations to provide or promote the ways of raising the standard of living of the masses that suffer injustice. We find ourselves in daily contact with those who have been rejected by society. Our first goal is to help these people achieve basic human development. We try to restore the sense of dignity that they should have as human beings, as well as children of the same Father. To accomplish this, we don't look first and see if they are dying or if they have a whole life ahead of them.

Q: Do you receive any aid from the Indian government?

MT: We do not receive any direct aid, but we have to recognize that the government helps us in a very effective way by the confidence, esteem, and respect they show us. This helps us in many ways, like getting land for the work we carry out and free transportation on the state railways.

Q: Do you receive any exemptions from the Indian government? Are you allowed to import everything freely?

MT: No, not everything, just food, medicines, medical equipment, clothing, and anything else that is needed for our work, such as furniture, typewriters, and sewing machines. We still need an import permit. We receive these things as gifts, and they all go to the poor. Nothing is for business transactions. It all goes to those in need, without regard to their race, beliefs, or religion. And there are so many in need! The only thing we have to do is declare to the government that these are free gifts. Since the government sees where everything goes, we are given the necessary permits. They realize that nothing goes into our pockets. Everything is given back to the poorest of the poor. That's why they trust us and give us the necessary permits.

Q: How do you manage what you receive?

MT: We have a register where we write down all our expenses, as well as what we receive and for what purpose we earmark these gifts. For example, if someone donates 100 rupees for the lepers, we don't use that money for anything else. We try to carry out the will of our donors.

Q: It seems that the Indian government is setting increasingly tighter restrictions on foreign missionaries. Are you affected by this?

MT: We are a native Indian institution. Our motherhouse is in India. So we don't fall under those restrictions. At the same time, we avoid evangelizing through means other than our work. Our works are our witness. If someone we help wants to become a Catholic, he has to see a priest. If there is a religious end to our work, it is nothing more than to bring all those we have contact with closer to God.

Q: Do you receive any help from others?

MT: Oh, yes! We have counted on the help of others since the very beginning. We call them co-workers. We have many kinds of co-workers, starting with the children from many countries who share their savings or the money they collect on drives for the children in India. Even though we Missionaries have the most visibility, really, we could carry out very little of our work without the generous help of thousands upon thousands of co-workers and friends throughout the world.

Q: Not all religious orders have known how to faithfully keep the initial spirit in which they were founded. Couldn't the Missionaries of Charity lose it also?

MT: Our fourth vow commits us to give free service to the poorest of the poor. This should keep us from the danger you mention. Our mission is so clear that there can be no misunderstandings. The poor know who they are and where they are. They are the reason for our order and our work. In Christ, they are the reason why we exist.

Q: Are you ever tempted with the idea of working among the rich, where everything would be easier for you?

MT: The poor are the reason for our existence. We were born for them and we dedicate ourselves just to them, without any temptation to turn away.

Q: What kind of growth have the Missionaries of Charity experienced?

MT: As I have said, we do not have a crisis in vocations. God is very generous with us and he sends us vocations. Among the young women who ask to join our order, there are those who are college-educated, while others come from the world of work. As for nationalities, the majority are Indian just as our order is. But there are also Irish, Italians, Germans, French, English, Spanish, Portuguese, and Americans. Also we have Sisters from Venezuela, Mexico, Peru, and Brazil. We even have a few from Africa and Australia.

Q: Do you attempt to present any special religious message through your work?

MT: Love has no other message but its own. Every day we try to live out Christ's love in a very tangible way in every one of our deeds. If we do any preaching, it is done with deeds, not with words. That is our witness to the Gospel.

Q: You need a lot of money to carry out your mission.

MT: Money is useful but the love, the attention, and the care we offer to others are the most important things. Love has to begin at home with those around us.

Q: Do you feel loved by the people?

MT: Yes, for the most part, even though the extreme conditions in which many of our people live keeps them from seeing our unconditional love. They see that we live among them and in poverty like they do. They appreciate that a lot. Still, not everything is peaceful all the time. Sometimes there are outbreaks of jealousy or impatience when we can't give them everything they need or ask for, or when they see that we are giving out the very things they want to others more needy than themselves. When that happens, we know it is useless to try to reason with them at that moment. It is best to allow them to calm down. They almost always have a change of attitude once they have calmed down.

Q: Do you witness conversions to Catholicism among the people you help?

MT: Yes, there are some conversions, but without us ever trying to encourage them directly. By practicing Christian love, we draw closer to God and we try to help others draw closer to him, without placing any religious pressure on anyone. When they accept love, they accept God and vice versa. Our witness is none other than that. At the same time it would be a mistake to forget that we find ourselves in India, among a people proud of their cultural and religious traditions. For that very reason they look with distrust upon any form of religious proselytism.

Q: What contact do the Missionaries of Charity have with their families?

MT: Once we are consecrated to serving the poor, they become our family. Naturally we do not deny our blood relationships with our biological families, but contact with them is very limited. Only under extraordinary circumstances, such as before leaving the country for a foreign mission, do we go home. We just cannot do it, first of all because of our poverty; we do not have the money to spend on trips. Second, none of us can leave our post of service and care to the sick, the dying, the lepers, and the orphans when they have no one else to look after them.

Q: What do you think of receiving awards?

MT: The same as always: I don't deserve them. I accept them willingly, not just to acknowledge the kindness of those who give the awards, but I think of what these awards can mean for our poor and our lepers. On the other hand, I think that these awards greatly help people to be favorably inclined towards the work we Missionaries of Charity carry out among the poorest of the poor.

Biographical Sketch of Mother Teresa

August 16, 1910: Mother Teresa is Born.

She is the daughter of Nikolle Bojaxhiu and Drana Bernai (of Italian descent), born in Skopje, capital of the Albanian republic of Macedonia. Mother Teresa is the third and last child of her parents. Her sister, Aga, was born in 1905 and her brother, Lazar, was born in 1907. Nikolle and Drana were married in 1900.

August 27, 1910: Mother Teresa is Baptized.

She is baptized in the parish church of the Sacred Heart of Jesus and given the name Gonxha (Agnes). Her parents are very devout Catholics, especially her mother.

1919: Her Father Dies.

Nikolle Bojaxhiu dies of an apparent poisoning after attending a political meeting. He was a municipal councilman with strong nationalist convictions.

1915-24: Schooling and Family Life.

Along with her brother and her sister, Agnes attends public school. She does well, even though her health is somewhat delicate. She also attends catechism classes at the parish, joins the parish choir, and belongs to a Catholic youth organization called the "Daughters of Mary." She has special interest in reading about missionaries and the lives of the saints.

Mother Teresa sums up her family life during her childhood and adolescence: "We were all very united, especially after the death of my father. We lived for each other and we made every effort to make one another happy. We were a very united and a very happy family."

Lazar, the only son, commented about the religious life of his mother and sisters: "We lived next to the parish church of the Sacred Heart of Jesus. Sometimes my mother and sisters seemed to live as much in the church as they did at home. They were always involved with the choir, the religious services, and missionary topics."

Lazar also commented about his mother's generosity: "She never allowed any of the many poor people who came to our door to leave empty handed. When we would look at her strangely, she would say, 'Keep in mind that even those who are not our blood relatives, even if they are poor, are still our brethren.' "

At the age of twelve, Agnes feels her first gentle calling to the religious and missionary life, a calling that will lie dormant for several years. Meanwhile, she continues being an active member of the "Daughters of Mary," as well as growing in her interest for missionary outreach with the encouragement of her parish priests, who are Jesuits. Agnes' brother, Lazar, moves to Austria to study to become a cavalry officer at the military academy there.

1928: A Calling to Join the Sisters of Our Lady of Loreto.

Agnes' interest in missionary outreach is confirmed by a clear calling to the religious life while she is praying before the altar of the Patroness of Skopje: "Our Lady interceded for me and helped me to discover my vocation." With the guidance and help of a Yugoslav Jesuit, Agnes applies for admission to the Order of the Sisters of Our Lady of Loreto (commonly called the Irish Ladies). She is attracted by their missionary work in India.

September 26, 1928: A Trip to the Mother House in Ireland.

Admitted provisionally, Agnes sets out on her trip to Dublin, traveling by train through Yugoslavia, Austria, Switzerland, France, and England until she arrives at the Mother House of the Sisters of Our Lady of Loreto.

December 1, 1928: Trip to Calcutta.

After two months of intensive English language studies, Agnes sets out by ship for India, where she arrives on January 6, 1929, after thirty-seven days.

Agnes stays in Calcutta only one week, after which she is sent to Darjeeling, in the foothills of the Himalayas, to begin her novitiate.

May 24, 1931: Temporary Vows.

After two years as a novice, Agnes professes temporary vows as a Sister of Our Lady of Loreto, changing her baptismal name for Teresa. "I chose the name Teresa for my religious vows. But it wasn't the name of the great Teresa of Avila. I chose the name of Teresa of the Little Flower, Therese of Lisieux."

1930-37: Sister Teresa in Calcutta.

After professing her temporary vows, Sister Teresa lives in Calcutta and serves as a geography and history teacher at St. Mary's School, run by the Sisters of Our Lady of Loreto.

May 24, 1937: Final Vows.

After renewing her temporary vows several times, Sister Teresa professes her final vows as a Sister of Our Lady of Loreto, and becomes a member of an order that was founded in the sixteenth century in England by Mary Ward.

Mother Teresa sums up very well her life in the religious order founded by Mary Ward: "I was the happiest nun at Loreto. I dedicated myself to teaching. That job, carried out for the love of God, was a true apostolate. I liked it very much." She becomes the director of studies at St. Mary's.

September 10, 1946: A Day of Inspiration.

That is what Mother Teresa calls it. She says, "While I was going by train from Calcutta to Darjeeling to participate in spiritual exercises, I was quietly praying when I clearly felt a call within my calling. The message was very clear. I had to leave the convent and consecrate myself to helping the poor by living among them. It was a command. I knew where I had to go, but I did not know how to get there.''

August 16, 1948: Permission from Rome to Pursue Her New Calling.

Leaving the Sisters of Our Lady of Loreto is difficult and painful for Sister Teresa. To do so, she needs special permission from Rome after an agreement is reached within her religious order. Finally, the permission is granted for her to live as a nun outside of the convent. She leaves on August 16, 1948, after taking off the religious habit of the Sisters of Our Lady of Loreto and putting on a white sari that looks like the ones worn by the poorest women in India. The sari has a blue border symbolizing her desire to imitate the Virgin Mary.

Mother Teresa leaves Calcutta to take an accelerated three-month course in basic nursing, then returns to put into practice her desire to dedicate herself to serving the poorest of the poor in the slums of Calcutta. This year she also applies for and is granted Indian citizenship, which she will retain throughout her life. Pope

Paul VI also grants her Vatican citizenship in the late 1970s to facilitate her missionary travels.

March 19, 1949: The First Follower of Mother Teresa in Her New Calling.

Subashini Das, an old student of Mother Teresa, visits her unexpectedly and says that she wants to join her. She will be the first nun of a religious order yet to exist.

July 10, 1950: The Order of Missionaries of Charity is Authorized by Rome.

Other young women follow Subashini Das at a promising rate. Mother Teresa says, "After 1949, I saw young women arriving one after another. All of them had been students of mine. They wanted to give everything to God and they were in a hurry to do so." On October 7, 1950, the feast of Our Lady of the Rosary, Rome authorizes the Order of the Missionaries of Charity. Ten women begin their novitiate which lasts two years.

August 22, 1952: The Home for Dying Destitutes Is Opened.

There are nearly thirty women in the order. A dozen of them have made their final vows.

There are twelve novices and the rest are postulants. The sisters are still in need of a convent of their own. They are "guests" in a rented flat, donated to them by Michael Gomes. They dedicate themselves to studies and religious formation, while caring for abandoned slum children and sick and dying destitutes.

Mother Teresa manages to acquire a home for the destitutes in Kalighat, a Hindu temple in the heart of Calcutta. The home is opened on August 22, 1952, the feast of Mary Immaculate, and is immediately filled to capacity, which it will always be through the years in spite of the constant "discharges" (there are always new admittances). The home is named *Nirmal Hriday*, "Home of the Pure Heart," a name that is just as acceptable to Hindus, who are the great majority of those who come to the home.

1953: The Mother House of the Missionaries of Charity Is Founded.

After "storming" heaven with constant prayers, the Missionaries of Charity are able to buy a home for their convent, located at 54 Lower Circular Road in Calcutta. The home is well located for their needs and temporarily spacious. The Mother House will become the central headquarters for the Missionaries of Charity.

Nearby, on the same street, the Sisters rent and later buy a home for abandoned and orphaned slum children. Many of the parents of these children have died in the Home for Dying Destitutes.

The Sisters initially want to open a home as well for the lepers that they care for. However, due to the opposition of the general population, they start up "mobile clinics" for the lepers. Later the Sisters will be able to open self-sufficient rehabilitation centers for lepers, called Titagahr and Shanti Nagar, on the outskirts of Calcutta.

1962: Mother Teresa Is Honored with Awards in Asia.

Mother Teresa is honored with the Padna Sri (Order of the Lotus) Award given to her by the Indian government and the Magsaysay Award given to her by the SEATO nations of southeastern Asia. She is declared the most worthy woman in Asia. However, in the West, she is still largely unknown.

February 1, 1965: The Missionaries of Charity Receive Further Recognition.

The Missionaries of Charity have now existed for fifteen years. They have had extraordinary growth and expansion. There are approximately three hundred sisters in the order and several homes. There are sisters of different European nationalities also. All of the Missionaries of Charity homes are still located in India under the jurisdiction of the local Catholic bishops. With the support of several bishops, Pope Paul VI decrees the praiseworthiness of the Missionaries of Charity, giving "validity" to the order for the wider Catholic church. This decree, along with an invitation from the Archbishop of Barquisimeto, Venezuela, to open a home in his diocese, enables the Missionaries of Charity to expand their missionary work.

1965-71: New Homes Are Opened Around the World.

The home in Venezuela is Mother Teresa's first home "abroad." During the following years more homes are opened in Africa, in Australia (Melbourne and Adelaide), in Europe (England and Italy) as a response to invitations extended by local Catholic bishops. The founding of the Missionaries of Charity's first home in Italy is in

Rome as a response to an invitation extended by Pope Paul VI, as Bishop of Rome. The Pope is an admirer and benefactor of Mother Teresa's work. By 1971 the Missionaries of Charity have fifty homes.

March 26, 1969: The Co-workers of the Missionaries of Charity Are Officially Established.

Mother Teresa's co-workers become a spiritual reality and an important element for furthering the work of the Missionaries of Charity. It is difficult, if not impossible, to ascertain their number due to their constant growth, as well as a certain carelessness of the Missionaries of Charity in keeping accurate statistics. There have been co-workers ever since the Missionaries of Charity were first founded. On March 3, 1969, Pope Paul VI approves the statutes for the co-workers and thereby they become officially affiliated with the Missionaries of Charity.

July 12, 1972: Mother Teresa's Mother, Drana Bernai, Dies.

Mother Teresa's mother dies in Albania. Her mother had wanted to leave Albania in order to see her daughter in India as well as her son, who lives in Sicily, before she died. The Albanian government refused to grant her permission to leave.

1974: Mother Teresa's Only Sister, Aga Bojaxhiu, Dies.

Mother Teresa's sister dies in Albania without having the opportunity to see either her sister or brother.

October 17, 1979: Mother Teresa Is Awarded the Nobel Peace Prize.

During the 1970s, the pen and microphone of Malcolm Muggeridge, a British journalist, make Mother Teresa famous in the West, not only in Catholic circles but in wider society. As a consequence, she is awarded the "Good Samaritan" Award in the United States, the "Templeton Award for Progress in Religion" in England, and the Pope John XXIII Peace Prize at the Vatican. On October 17, 1979, Mother Teresa is awarded the most famous international award: the Nobel Peace Prize. Nevertheless, her habitual simplicity and humility are not altered.

December 10, 1979: Mother Teresa Accepts the Nobel Peace Prize.

Mother Teresa accepts her award from the

hands of King Olaf V of Norway, in the name of the poor whom she represents and to whom she has dedicated her life.

1980-85: The Missionaries of Charity Open Many New Homes and Are Blessed with Many New Vocations.

In 1980 there are fourteen homes outside of India in places as diverse as Lebanon, West Germany, Yugoslavia, Mexico, Brazil, Peru, Kenya, Haiti, Spain, Ethiopia, Belgium, New Guinea, and Argentina. After the Nobel Peace Prize is awarded, the Missionaries of Charity's rate of expansion is surprising: eighteen new homes are opened in 1981, twelve in 1982, and fourteen in 1983. The Missionaries of Charity are also blessed with an increasing rate of new vocations, making the order an exception in an era of general decline in the number of new vocations for religious orders.

1986-89: The Order Enters Countries Previously Closed to Missionaries.

The Missionaries of Charity are allowed to open homes in countries where the doors were previously closed to missionaries: Ethiopia and Southern Yemen. Also they are allowed to come to Nicaragua, Cuba, and Russia, where atheism is actively promoted by the state. In the case of the Soviet Union, one of the fruits of Mikhail Gorbachev's "perestroika" has been permission for Mother Teresa to open a home in Moscow.

February 1986: Pope John Paul II Comes to Calcutta.

The Pope visits Mother Teresa and sees first-hand the work of the Missionaries of Charity.

May 21, 1988: A Home at the Vatican.

The Missionaries of Charity open a shelter for the homeless in Rome at the Vatican. It is called "A Gift from Mary" to commemorate the Marian Year. The shelter has seventy-two beds for men and women and two dining halls, one for residents and one for those who stop in. The shelter also has a lounge, an infirmary, and a patio which faces the Pope Paul VI audience hall.

1988-89: Mother Teresa Is Hospitalized Twice.

Due to heart trouble, Mother Teresa is hospitalized twice. It is not the first time that she has overextended herself to the point of physical exhaustion and been hospitalized. Even the Pope asks her to take better care of her health. Her doctors install a pacemaker and order her to take six months of rest.

April 16, 1990: Mother Teresa Steps Down as the Superior General of the Missionaries of Charity.

Citing ill health as the main reason, Mother Teresa steps down as the Superior General of her order. Relieved of her responsibilities, she is able to spend more time traveling and visiting various houses of Sisters.

September 1990: Mother Teresa Is Called out of Retirement and Re-elected as the Superior General of the Missionaries of Charity.

Recognizing her unique spiritual genius and leadership of the order, the Sisters of the Missionaries of Charity re-elect Mother Teresa as Superior General, even though she is now eighty years of age and in ill health.

Notes

TWO
The Family and the Poor

1. This material is from an address given by Mother Teresa at the World Congress on the Family, which was held July 21, 1986 at Paray-le-Monial, France. In this address, Mother Teresa focuses on the family's call to serve the poor, the importance of family prayer, and the lack of love in modern family life—especially in the West.

2. Joy is one of the constant and dominant themes of Mother Teresa's spirituality. Who has not felt drawn to know how she understands joy?

   In the Rule of the Missionaries of Charity, there is an explanation. Joy is described as an undeniable gift of the Holy Spirit and a sign of the kingdom of God. Christ wanted to share his joy with his apostles: May my joy be in you and may it be complete (John 15:11). Joy was also Our Lady's strength. Only joy and gratitude to God could enable her to go in haste into the hill country of Judea to help her cousin Elizabeth.

   Joy is a sure sign of prayer. It is a sign of our generosity and intimate and constant union with God.

   God is love. A joyful heart is the natural

consequence of a heart inflamed with love, since the one who gives joyfully gives more. Joy is a net of love within which one can catch souls. A Sister overflowing with joy preaches without needing words.

For the Missionaries of Charity, joy is a necessity and their strength, even from a physical point of view, since it makes them constantly available to serve others. The best way to show gratitude to God and to others is to accept everything joyfully. A joyful Sister is a reflection of God's love and of hope for eternal happiness, a flame of consuming love.

THREE
Our Life with Christ

1. Love and the desire to serve Christ in the poor is something so essential for the Missionaries of Charity that Mother Teresa has said, "If there are poor people on the moon, we will go there." It is said that when Mother Teresa was in Cuba in 1986 and visited Fidel Castro, she expressed her desire to open a home for the poorest of the poor in Havana. Castro said, "That is impossible. We have no poor here." Mother Teresa responded, "Very well, but there must be sick, dying, and disabled people." "Certainly," answered Castro. "Well then," said Mother Teresa, "we would like to take care of them." The Missionaries of Charity now have two homes in Cuba. The first one opened in November 1987 in Havana, and the second one

was opened at the end of 1988 in the interior of the island.

FOUR
We Are the Children of God

1. This material is drawn from Mother Teresa's address to French children and their parents at the World Congress on the Family, which was held on July 21, 1986 at Paray-le-Monial, France. In this address, she encourages the children to serve and love others, especially their own family members and the poor in their midst. She also thanks parents who have given their children to the priesthood and the religious life.

2. In an interview, Mother Teresa expanded on this particular insight into the Blessed Virgin Mary's visitation to her cousin Elizabeth, and the greeting of the unborn child in Elizabeth's womb: "It occurred to me a few days ago that the first person to recognize and welcome Jesus was a little child who was still in his mother's womb. That little child lept for joy when his mother, St. Elizabeth, greeted Mary, who was expecting Jesus. It was a little unborn child who was the first one to receive Jesus. And he not only welcomed him, he rejoiced since the Scriptures tell us that he lept for joy in his mother's womb."

   In addressing the issue of abortion, Mother Teresa frequently turns to this scriptural insight, pointing out how the unborn baby in Elizabeth's womb responds to God's Word as a *person*.

3. One should not take Mother Teresa's statistics as exact, due to the constant change of circumstances tending towards serving greater rather than lesser numbers of people. Moreover, Mother Teresa is among those who least worry about statistics. She has repeatedly expressed that what matters is not how much work is accomplished but how much love is put into the work.

4. When they profess their vows before the community, this is what the Missionaries of Charity pray: "In the name of the Father, and of the Son, and of the Holy Spirit, amen. In honor of and for the glory of God, and moved only by the desire to quench the infinite thirst for souls of Jesus on the cross, I consecrate myself entirely to him in full surrender and loving trust, here and now, at the hands of my superior. I make my vows of chastity, poverty, obedience, and whole-hearted, free service to the poorest of the poor, in accordance with the Statutes of the Missionaries of Charity. I surrender myself whole-heartedly to this religious family, so that by the grace of the Holy Spirit and with the help of the Immaculate Heart of Mary, the cause of our joy and Queen of the world, I may be brought into perfect love for God and my neighbor, and may make the church fully present in the world today.

5. "Whole-hearted, free service" is a specific vow professed by the Missionaries of Charity, which is explained in their literature concerning their

mission, as follows: "*Service*—to be always willing to offer humble, loving service to the best of one's abilities to the poorest of the poor, not only with the simple intention of helping them, but also for the love of God; to share, person to person, through our presence and speech the over-flowing abundance of God's love, which we experience in our own lives." "*Whole-hearted*—to give all that we can, without considering the cost, until it hurts to the poorest of the poor; not only our hands in service, our lips to speak, and our eyes to see, but also our hearts to love with kindness, humility, and joy." "*Free*—to give joy-fully what has been received without expecting any money, goods, gratitude, or appreciation."

FIVE
In the Very Heart of the World

1. The requirements for a young woman to have a vocation as a Missionary of Charity are the following: She must be at least eighteen years of age, free of any impediments (according to canon law), have right intentions, and good spiritual and physical health that will enable her to withstand the hardships of this special vocation. She must also have an ability to learn, especially the languages of the countries where she may be sent, a pleasant personality, and sound judgment.

2. Mother Teresa mentions the schedule of the Mother House, the most important home of her

order, located at 54 Lower Circular Road in Calcutta. The schedules of the other homes are based on this one, with some slight variations to accommodate the particular demands of the locality where these homes are found.

SIX
The Need for Holy Priests

1. This talk was given to a gathering of priests attending the World Congress on the Family on July 21, 1986 in Paray-le-Monial, France. In this address, Mother Teresa stresses the need for holy priests because of their important role in the church, especially because of their sacramental powers in making the eucharistic and forgiving Christ present to his people.

    The Missionaries of Charity make a special point of interceding for priests and for priestly vocations.

2. Three homes were established in Southern Yemen: Hodeida (1973), Taiz (1974), and Sanaa (1976).

3. Ordinarily, the prerequisite for the founding of any home by the Missionaries of Charity is that an agreement be reached with the local Catholic bishop, so the order is assured that the Sisters will receive the following spiritual assistance: daily Mass, confession every two weeks, a talk on a religious topic every two weeks (not indispens-

able), and a chapel in their home with permission to have daily adoration of the Blessed Sacrament.

SEVEN
To Be Jesus

1. This prayer and "Make Me a Channel of Your Peace," attributed to St. Francis of Assisi, are Mother Teresa's favorites. They have both been incorporated into the daily devotions of her order. In the case of the prayer by Cardinal Newman, the Missionaries of Charity pray it every day at the end of Mass.

2. Mother Teresa gave this address to six thousand priests in Rome at the Basilica of Santa Sabina on October 9, 1984. The address was part of a spiritual retreat Mother Teresa gave for Rome's priests, at the invitation of Pope John Paul II. In this stirring retreat talk, Mother Teresa encourages priests to be the presence of Christ in the world—to be holy and consecrated to God in every situation.

EIGHT
The Poor Can Teach Us

1. Since 1987, Mother Teresa's work has included a movement (for the movement has only been recognized at the diocesan level and therefore is only a local outreach) called the Lay Missionaries

of Charity. This movement is defined as an international association of lay single people and married couples who profess private vows of (conjugal) chastity, poverty, obedience, and whole-hearted, free service to the poorest of the poor, according to their state in life. They live a life of prayer and a spirit of joyful sacrifice in the heart of their families and the world. Moreover, they are spiritually affiliated with the Missionaries of Charity. The specific goal of the Lay Missionaries of Charity is to quench the thirst of Christ on the cross for the love of souls. Their special mission is to work for the salvation and sanctification of their own family members, as well as that of the poorest of the poor throughout the world.

NINE
Sharing the Good News

1. Here and elsewhere throughout this book, opposition to abortion and heartfelt concern for the children and women involved are key themes of Mother Teresa's most recent addresses and writings. It is important to clarify here what becomes apparent when the entire book is read: namely, Mother Teresa does not simply speak against abortion and other modern evils, she acts on her principles. In the case of abortion, that action has taken the shape of opening orphanages for unwanted children and homes for unwed mothers throughout the world, under the auspices of the Missionaries of Charity. Further,

in an attempt to address the problem at an earlier stage, Mother Teresa's Missionaries of Charity are also trained to teach poor married couples—especially in Third World countries like India—Natural Family Planning, which is approved by the Catholic church.

TEN

Carrying God's Love to Others

1. In April of 1982, Mother Teresa attended a conference in Japan on the world's population. She took the occasion to address the Japanese co-workers of the Missionaries of Charity. This is an excerpt of her remarks to the co-workers. (See note following for an explanation of the co-workers and their role as helpers of the Missionaries of Charity.)

2. Like many addresses Mother Teresa gives throughout the world, this excerpt of her speech in Japan focuses in particular on the call of the co-workers of the Missionaries of Charity. The term co-worker refers to the work that these helpers of the Missionaries of Charity carry out. There are hundreds of thousands of co-workers—not to be confused with the Lay Missionaries of Charity who profess the same four vows as the Missionaries of Charity. The co-workers are governed by a statute approved by Pope Paul IV and are an inter-religious group of men and women of good will. In fact, a large number of co-workers are not

Christians, but Buddhists and Muslims. This is possible because the basic requirement for being a co-worker is simply to recognize God in each human being and to have the desire to serve him in the poorest of the poor. The service is in direct relationship with the possibilities and circumstances of each co-worker.

Mother Teresa has confessed that she has a certain preference for the sick, even physically handicapped, co-workers, whose help consists of, and is almost always limited to, praying and offering their sufferings to God. Considered novel is Mother Teresa's restriction that co-workers not be charged a membership fee nor organize fundraising events. She believes and teaches that their first priority is the sanctification of their own lives. They are to carry out the most ordinary and least attention-getting tasks: "Those things," she says, "that nobody seems to have time to do." She does not restrict their giving, and she even recommends that they give until it hurts. But more than outward giving, she encourages them to give whole-heartedly and freely of their very selves.

ELEVEN
Love Changes Hearts

1. Besides these four vows, there are also six levels of commitment in the formation process of becoming a lifelong member of the order. This formation process extends over nine-and-a-half years and

involves these levels: 1) *aspirant* (six months)—the candidate is given the opportunity to see the life and work of the Missionaries of Charity; 2) *postulant* (one year)—allows time for the order and the candidate to get acquainted; 3) *novice* (two years)—helps the individual fully understand and begin to live the life of a Missionary of Charity, so the individual clearly understands the vocation; 4) *temporary vows* (five years)—deepens the Sister's religious commitment and further prepares her for the apostolate and mission work of the order; 5) *final preparation* (one year)—a special period of renewal and preparation immediately before the Sister in question makes her final vows; 6) *final vows* (life-time formation)—Missionaries of Charity are taught that training and formation are not over when the final vows have been professed. Besides receiving ongoing formation, there is a special time of renewal, usually ten years after profession of final vows.

TWELVE
The Hands and Feet of Jesus

1. Mother Teresa's words after receiving the Discovery Award from Marquette University on June 13, 1981. Inspired by the very name of the award, Fr. Bruce Biever, S.J., vice-president of Marquette University, called Mother Teresa "a discoverer and explorer who has shown the light of God's love in an age of cynicism and hopelessness, and explored the regions of our needs that

are not found on any map by giving and receiving the love of Christ.''

The Jesuit priest added that the presence of Mother Teresa of Calcutta gives us the opportunity to recognize new dimensions in discovery that remind all humanity of God's never-ending kindness and love. He also said that the joy felt by the poorest of the poor and the dying destitutes in Mother Teresa and her Sister's care represent a window through which one can get a glimpse of a new world.

Fr. Biever's comments touched on the heart of Mother Teresa's work, showing that her love leads the abandoned and dying to discover again the dimensions of hope and joy. By her life and example, people from all nations have the opportunity to discover that God's light still shines in our times with new radiance.

THIRTEEN
God Loves Children

1. This material is taken from an address which Mother Teresa gave at the World Congress on the Family at Paray-le-Monial, France on July 21, 1986. Mother Teresa spoke to a group of French children and encouraged them to love Jesus and the poor; she also expressed the hope that some of them would become Missionaries of Charity.

   It is interesting to note that of all the countries in Europe, after Poland, France is the one that has given the greatest number of vocations to the Missionaries of Charity.

EIGHTEEN
Seeing, Loving, and Serving Christ in the Poor

1. This interview summarizes a couple of encounters between Mother Teresa and the editor, from approximately June 1976 to June 1980.

NOTE TO THE READER: Where no source is listed for a particular chapter, the omission is because the material has been drawn from many different sources and then combined into chapter form by the editor.

Other Books of Interest
by Mother Teresa

Jesus, The Word to Be Spoken

Let the words and example of Mother Teresa of Calcutta
lead you each day into a closer relationship with God.
This pocket guide to daily prayer and meditation is rich
spiritual fare for all who are serious about following
Jesus Christ. *$5.99*

Heart of Joy

These are the writings and teachings of a woman whose
works and words have touched more people than any
other woman living today. *$5.99*

One Heart Full of Love

More stirring addresses and interviews given by Mother
Teresa to her Missionaries of Charity and other groups
worldwide on such topics as self-giving, the call to love
our neighbor, and spiritual poverty in the West. *$5.99*